# ENGLISH POETRY
## AND THE
# ENGLISH LANGUAGE

# ENGLISH POETRY
## AND THE
# ENGLISH LANGUAGE

BY

F. W. BATESON

New York

RUSSELL & RUSSELL

1961

*We had perswaded him to publish a Discourse concerning Style. In this he had design'd to deduce all down to the particular use of the English Genius and Language.*

THOMAS SPRAT
An Account of the Life and Writings of
Mr. Abraham Cowley, 1668

# PREFACE TO SECOND EDITION

I HAVE suppressed in this edition my original rather gawky sub-title ("An Experiment in Literary History") and with it the polemical preface in which I explained what it was all about. At that time (1934) I was in the middle of editing *The Cambridge Bibliography of English Literature*, an ambitious work of reference which had enrolled contributors from most of the university English Departments as well as dozens of independent scholars. The crass philistinism of "research" in those distant days was a constant shock to me. On the other hand, when I turned to critics I especially admired—T. S. Eliot, for example, or William Empson —I was conscious of a pseudo-scholarship which in my youthful self-righteousness I found not less shocking. But the literary situation has changed in these respects since 1934. My polemics, if they were ever justified, would now be irrelevant. We are in general agreement to-day that the literary critic must try and get his facts right, and that the literary historian must begin to know the difference—even with his eyes bandaged, as it were— between writing that is good and less good. The two *principles* are accepted, though we shall continue to wrangle naturally about their application.

But what *is* the literary fact? The hypothesis I proposed in 1934—and to which I still adhere—is that the ultimate or fundamental literary fact is a verbal artifact, more or less linguistically complex, which is "published" (communciated) at a particular time in a particular historical society. Some verbal artifacts have, of course, proved more memorable than others, a condition that the hypothesis attributes to a greater coincidence between their language and the language spoken by their original audiences. In a sense, according to the hypothesis, the language writes the literature. (The English poetical classics are what they are, as I try to demonstrate in the chapters that follow, because of their authors' special sensitivity to the potentialities of the English language in their time.)

In order to understand the poetry, a prerequisite to assessing it critically, we must know the history of the changing fortunes of the English language. That is the innocent-looking basic proposition. But to know a language is not just a matter of digging in dictionaries and grammars. A language is partly what its best speakers think it is (hence the importance of recovering and clarifying the pronouncements of representative figures), and it is also, awaiting the analysis of the future, the general characteristics and trends implicit in it at any one time. Here, in this general framework of changing linguistic structure and emphasis, the literary fact too is most often to be found. For, except provisionally, in the psychological laboratory, language is never separable from meaning, just as meanings are never separable from values. (Hard words perhaps, but the modern philosophers seem to have demonstrated that they are true.) This is not to deny that *behind* language, meanings and values there is usually an individual writer and also a society in which the writer has grown up and whose language he employs. But these human factors are the artifact's context, its causes or its effects; they are not the poem itself, which is a verbal construct, a changing pattern (as I argue) of repetitive linguistic devices that is also a compound of the very best contemporary words in the very best contemporary order.

As it was originally presented my hypothesis was challenged by F. R. Leavis in a long review in *Scrutiny*, which has been reprinted, with my equally long retort and Dr. Leavis's reply to it, in *The Importance of Scrutiny*, edited by Eric Bentley (1948). René Wellek has also questioned some of my contentions in *Theory of Literature* (1949). I am grateful to them for opening my eyes to some difficulties I had overlooked. The argument is continued and extended in my *English Poetry: a Critical Introduction* (1950), and a book I have now in preparation to be called *Good English* will work out more fully the theoretical implications of the hypothesis.

I had hoped at one time to revise and amplify *English Poetry and the English Language*, so as to bring it up to date. But an experimental re-writing of the first chapter has demonstrated that a hiatus of nearly thirty years cannot be decently bridged by patchwork interpolations. A proper revision would mean writing a new and perhaps less coherent book. Some changes and corrections have, however, been introduced, and I have added a short index. If it had been possible I would also have liked to incorporate in chapter II parts of Richard Foster Jones's *The Triumph of the English language* (1953), and references to several other recent books and articles would have been desirable. Nevertheless the story told in these pages is still, I believe, substantially correct. I did not realize in 1934 that W. H. Auden was soon to become an American citizen, though I remain more than

ever convinced that his earlier verse has been the principal liberating force of modern poetry in England. To
the question I raise on p. 122, "who is to be our Dryden?", the answer has clearly been Auden. No doubt
Yeats and Eliot do deserve something better than the
disparaging footnote they get on p. 128, but I suspect
that history will confirm the general tenor of that verdict.
Splendid poets though they both are (Dylan Thomas
might be added here), they are outside the central English poetic tradition; there is nothing the contemporary
English poet can usefully learn from them, as he can
learn in their different ways from Robert Graves or
Empson or Philip Larkin—or (supremely) from Auden.
And this is surely because modern English, "British
English", has after all a severity and a decorum far
tougher and far more pervasive than it is usual to accord
it, against which Celtic rhetoric and American experimentalism have hitherto broken in vain. I hope to
present the evidence in full in due course.

OXFORD, May, 1961                          F. W. B.

# CONTENTS

# I

# INTRODUCTION

In Sir Arthur Quiller-Couch's *Studies in Literature* (1919) there is a lecture entitled ' "Classical" and "Romantic" ', which includes a devastating 'Short History of English Literature' in 400 words. The period from the Renaissance to the present day, the poetry of which is to be the subject of this 'experiment' of mine, is summarized as follows :

Italianate Revival: French Pleiad: Influence producing Wyat and Surrey: School of Wyat and Surrey. The Renaissance, The New Learning: Columbus discovers America. Surprise at this. Sir Thomas More at home in Chelsea. Simultaneous rise of the Drama. Evolution of the Miracle Play. The Miracle Play superseded by the Morality. Evolution of the Drama. Evolution of Blank Verse. Shakespeare—his Comedies—his Tragedies—his Historical plays—his indebtedness to his times—his many-sidedness—his Will—his second-best bed—his romanticism. Classicism of Ben Jonson. Reaction (metaphysical) led by Donne. The mystical school. The Platonical school. Milton's indebtedness to the Copernican system. Tendency of Waller, Dryden, Pope. Decline of metaphysical school. Rise of the classical school. Tyranny of the Pamphlet, rise of the Essay, rise of the Novel. Tendency to write like Gray, or Collins : tendency to admire Dr. Johnson : tendency not to admire Dr. Johnson so much—tendency to make up on the swings what you have lost on the roundabouts : tendency to be Cowper or Crabbe : all these tendencies culminating in Romantic revolt. Naturalism (*alias* Wordsworth), mysticism (*alias* Coleridge), deism (*alias* Shelley), the revolutionary spirit (*alias* Byron), and sensuous naturalism (*alias* Keats).

Exhaustion of tendencies. Reform Act of 1832—its devastating influence on English Literature, and especially on its study in Cambridge. Albeit we have heard it rumoured that in a later generation Tennyson, Browning, Carlyle, Ruskin, Arnold, Morris, and others made a spirited attempt to revive the interplay of those tendencies and reactions which we have been considering, at this point we down the curtain and count the takings.

Sir Arthur's parody is the epitaph of what I may call the Authorized Version of the history of English literature. No one will ever attempt now to retrace the progress of English poetry in terms of ' schools ', ' influences ', ' revivals ', ' revolts ', ' tendencies ', and ' reactions '. The -isms and -ations are utterly and finally discredited. But if there are to be no more ' influences ' and ' tendencies ' it is worth asking what is to take their place. Is there an alternative ? Sir Arthur's answer would appear to be, Yes, the alternative is literary criticism. The pageant of literature is, to him, simply ' the product of successive men of genius and talent '. ' It is the pure loveliness of it that alone should concern you.' It is because I am not entirely satisfied with this answer, because I believe a history of literature still possible, that I have written this book. A list of ' successive men of genius and talent ' is as meaningless to me as a biographical dictionary—a mere handful of beads without a string on which to thread them. It is permissible to demand something more. The English poets are not suspended in a vacuum. They have relations and connexions both with each other and with the general life of their times, and it should

be possible to illustrate and define those inter-con-
nexions without falling into the verbose inanities of
'influences' and 'tendencies'.[1]

But it will first be necessary to examine with more
precision than is usual the whole notion of 'literary
history' in its bearing upon poetry.

I

Literary history, whatever it is, is not a department of literary criticism. Ideally, indeed, the two
activities do not even overlap ; the one is the *com-
plement* of the other. They bear, that is, the same
relation to each other that the science of organic
chemistry bears to biology : the subject-matter and
method are the same, the difference is in the initial
assumptions involved.

[1] W. J. Courthope, whose elaborate *History of English Poetry* (1895–
1910) is the only history of the subject that *is* a history, complained
with justice that 'what is often meant by a History of English Poetry
is merely an account of the lives of the English poets, and such an esti-
mate of their works as may be formed by the judgement of the particular historians'. The charge remains true to-day. That attractive work
*The English Muse* (1933), by Professor Oliver Elton, is a recent example
of the kind of thing Courthope protested against. 'There is such a
thing', Professor Elton begins, 'as the English spirit, and it is mirrored
in our poetry. The melancholy of the *Seafarer* might be detected in
some of Conrad's inarticulate British sailors ; chivalry is the same in
*Maldon*, in the *Battle of Otterburn*, and in the *Lady of the Lake*. There
is a true continuity of spirit, as well as of expression, in our poetry.
Dream of it for a moment as all written by a single poet of unimaginable gifts, and older than Methuselah.' There is, of course, no reason
why Professor Elton should not dream that English poetry is all written
by a single poet of unimaginable gifts. But such dreams cannot possibly,
by any stretching of language, be called literary history. They *may* be
literary criticism.

Literary history presupposes by the fact of its existence a process of change. If the writings of one generation did not differ, in one important respect or another, from those of the next generation it could not exist at all. Whatever superstructure therefore he may add later, the literary historian begins as the mere recorder of literary variation. He is not, of course, restricted to the differences between generations. Every writer, every book even, may concern him. 'What happens when a new work of art is created is something that happens simultaneously to all the works of art which preceded it. The existing monuments form an ideal order among themselves, which is modified by the introduction of the new (the really new) work of art among them.'[1]

But a limitation is implicit in this principle. A writer who is not 'really new', who seems only to repeat the successes of others, is beyond the scope of literary history except in so far as his repetitions are incomplete. And novelty and literary merit are not always synonymous. 'There is nothing in the drama of Rotrou', says Brunetière, 'which is not to be found in that of Corneille; if the work of the former did not exist, there would be nothing lacking to the history of our theatre, and that is why his tragi-comedies may interest a few of the curious, but have not a place in the history of French literature.'[2] The judgement is typical of the immorality of the literary historian. Rotrou was not, as it

---

[1] T. S. Eliot, *The Sacred Wood*, 1920, p. 44.
[2] Quoted by P. H. Frye, *Romance and Tragedy*, 1922, p. 10.

happens, a mere imitator; and his plays would not have been worse, or very different, if Corneille had never been born. Corneille was an accident. But Brunetière's injustice was inevitable. The only values the literary historian can acknowledge, *qua* literary historian, are *differences*, and the stage in the evolution of the French drama that Rotrou might have represented was already occupied by Corneille.

A literary critic would not have been tempted by such a simplification. For literary criticism, unlike literary history, stresses the similarities, not the differences, between one writer and another. The basic assumption, indeed, of the critic is that works of literature, whatever their form or origin, are always ultimately *comparable*. Matthew Arnold, it will be remembered, recommended the 'lines and expressions of the great masters' as a 'touchstone' to other poetry. 'If we have any tact we shall find them, when we have lodged them well in our minds, an infallible touchstone for detecting the presence or absence of high poetic quality, and also the degree of this quality, in all other poetry which we may place beside them.'[1] But a touchstone is simply a standard of comparison. Chaucer and Burns could both be compared with Dante, because (to Arnold as a literary critic) Chaucer, Burns, and Dante, in spite of superficial differences, were fundamentally the *same*. To the critic *all* literature, in so far as it is literature, is fundamentally the same. Dante is identical with Homer and Aristophanes with Rabelais. The differences don't matter ; the resem-

[1] 'The Study of Poetry' (*Essays in Criticism. Second Series,* 1888).

blances are the thing. And so, if literary history is primarily concerned with the exception, literary criticism is primarily concerned with the rule. The standards the critic applies and the judgements he delivers derive from those ideals of good writing that every writer, in every language and period, has always acknowledged and aspired to. It follows that whereas literary history presupposes a process of change, literary criticism presupposes a static condition, a virtual changelessness in literature. Mr. E. M. Forster has recommended the student of the novel to visualize 'all the novelists writing their novels at once'. Henry James sits by Richardson, H. G. Wells by Dickens, Sterne by Virginia Woolf. 'All through history', he continues, 'writers while writing have felt more or less the same. They have entered a common state which it is convenient to call inspiration, and, having regard to that state, we may say that History develops, Art stands still.'[1]

Mr. Forster was speaking as a critic. Art, considered as the subject-matter of criticism, does stand still. But art may also be considered as history, and as history it cannot stand still. It develops every decade, often every year, and it is only by virtue of these developments that it becomes the concern of the historian. If there is something in common in the novels of Henry James and Richardson, there is also quite obviously something distinguishable, something that they have not in common. And the business of the literary historian, while always employing the tools and accepting the hier-

[1] *Aspects of the Novel*, 1927, p. 35.

archies of the literary critic, is to isolate, define, and explain that 'something not in common'.

The literary historian's initial assumption, then, is that literature is changing and heterogeneous. But this assumption is qualified by a second assumption. For literature's changes, considered simply as changes, are meaningless. A flux, and it is under that aspect that literature presents itself first of all to the literary historian, is unintelligible except in reference to something outside itself. The historian must therefore assume, if he is to produce a history and not a chronicle, not a mere sequence of names and dates, that some pattern is discernible in the flux of literature's varieties. Every book *must* be relatable to a particular literary tradition; its divergences from that tradition *must* be explicable. But such relations and explanations can only be determined by a standard of comparison that is outside the flux. And so the historian is compelled to correlate the temporal sequence with which he begins, literature's mere irrational changes, with some causal sequence (e.g. the science of economics). Without such assistance he will be simply unintelligible. But the discoveries to which he then proceeds and the judgements which he pronounces will inevitably be conditioned by the nature of the science he has called to his aid. (A history of poetry of which the basis is economics will be restricted to those aspects of poetry which are visible to the economist's eye.) It follows that a literary history can never be wholly disinterested or complete. What does not follow is that every mode of interpretation—economic, racial, evolutionary, religious, philosophical, psycho-analytic—must necessarily be equally legitimate. It would be possible to write a *medical* history of literature, in which its development was interpreted in terms of the comparative healthiness of different periods and localities. It would be possible—but it would not be worth while. The crucial problem that confronts the would-be historian of literature is to select the mode of interpretation that *is* worth while.

Leslie Stephen, following in the footsteps of Taine, has pleaded the claims of a sociological version of literary history :

If we allow ourselves to contemplate a philosophical history, which shall deal with the causes of events and aim at exhibiting the evolution of human society, we should see that the history of literature would be a subordinate element of the whole structure. The political, social, ecclesiastical and economical factors, and their complex actions and reactions, would all have to be taken into account. The literary historian would be concerned with the ideas that find utterance through the poet and philosopher, and with the constitution of the class which at any time forms the literary organ of society. The critic who deals with the individual work would find such knowledge necessary to a full appreciation of his subject; and conversely, the appreciation would in some degree help the labourer in other departments of history to understand the nature of the forces which are governing the social development. However far we may be from such a consummation and reluctant to indulge in the magniloquent language which it suggests, I imagine that a literary history is so far satisfactory as it takes the facts into consideration and regards literature, in the perhaps too pretentious phrase, as a particular function of the whole social organism.

I have borrowed this quotation from Professor P. H. Frye's *Romance and Tragedy* (1922), and I shall make use of Professor Frye's refutation of it.

At best [Professor Frye points out] society is but the condition, and like all conditions, does not originate but influences. To say nothing of the merely empirical objection that it is often the author who is, in all seeming, the first to divine and rescue truth and is frequently obliged to impose himself upon his audience if he would be heard at all, so that he appears rather to form his public than to be formed by it—it is evident, in addition, that a work of literature in the strict sense of the word is something exceptional by its very nature. It is the difference—or as we still say, rather condescendingly, the genius—which gives the book its value. Only the contribution, the distinctively personal vision, is of any permanent importance—and it is the work of permanent importance alone which is properly literature, since literature is obviously literature by virtue of its message to us who read it and not by virtue of its expression of local and temporal peculiarities.

Professor Frye's argument is, I believe, unanswerable. But Professor Frye does not seem to be aware of the real deadliness of his criticism of the sociological school. It is the work, he says, of permanent importance alone which is properly literature. And who, the sociologist may retort, is Professor Frye to decide what works are alone of permanent importance? The answer to this is that it is not just a question of Professor Frye's word against Leslie Stephen's. Professor Frye has appealed from literary history to literary criticism. His objection to regarding literature as a function of the social organism is the literary critic's objection—not that it cannot be done, but that it can only be done by disregarding those elements in literature that distinguish good writing from bad. In the last resort, therefore, the literary historian stands or falls only in so far as he satisfies, or fails to satisfy, the literary critic. If the interpretation he proposes does not clarify the central and universal significance of the literature he is treating, it is worthless. His history may be excellent social history or economic history, but there is one thing it will not be : it will not be *literary* history.

Professor Frye, who is an American and a pupil of Irving Babbitt, wishes to replace the sociology of Taine and Leslie Stephen by what he calls 'universal ideas and principles'. 'In a single breath,' he says, 'what we need is a fundamental literary criticism which shall differ from philology and history in being a criticism of principles and from aesthetics in devoting itself to the peculiarities of literature as distinct from the fine arts—that is to say, as a medium of ideas.' What are Professor Frye's 'ideas'? The word is vague and can be used in a variety of senses. (The *Oxford Dictionary* recognizes eleven distinct meanings and various subdivisions.) Professor Frye, however, whatever his other shortcomings may be, is not vague. He knows what he wants to say, and by an 'idea' he makes it quite plain that he means an 'ideal', an ethical principle. The subject of his able and provocative essay on

'Shakespeare and Sophocles' is, he says, 'the divergence between the kinds of thing that they stand for'. One would have thought the kinds of thing Shakespeare and Sophocles stand for was *Antony and Cleopatra* and the *Oedipus Coloneus*, and Professor Frye does refer once to the second of these plays. But they are not what interests him in Shakespeare and Sophocles. 'They personify', he continues, 'two diverse and inimical ideals of life and literature. Aside from what is eternal and timeless in them both, the one is modern, the other ancient. And as far as these categories are significant, modern is to be understood, by the light of its genealogy, in the sense of popular and natural; ancient in that of humane and moral.'

Now this sort of thing is all very well as far as it goes, but the crude fact is that it does not go as far as literature. What are we to think of a theory of literary history that deliberately excludes what is 'eternal and timeless' in literature? 'It is the work of permanent importance alone', to quote Professor Frye himself, 'which is properly literature, since literature is obviously literature by virtue of its message to us who read it and not by virtue of its expression of local and temporal peculiarities.' Moreover, the ideals that Shakespeare and Sophocles personify have nothing whatever to do with their merits either as dramatists or poets. Mr. T. S. Eliot has said the last word upon this subject. 'In truth,' Mr. Eliot remarks in the course of a discussion of *Shakespeare and the Stoicism of Seneca*, 'neither Shakespeare nor Dante did any real thinking—that was not their job; and the relative value of the thought current at their time, the material enforced upon each to use as the vehicle of his feeling, is of no importance.' Poetry is not made out of 'universal ideas and principles'. If these things are occasionally to be found embedded in poetry, the fact is poetically an accident which does not affect the writer's status one way or another. 'Novelists and poets, *qua* novelists and poets, do not really have ideas at all, they have perceptions, intuitions, emotional convictions.'[1]

[1] J. Middleton Murry, *The Problem of Style*, 1922, p. 6.

I may seem at this point to be sheltering myself behind the authority of Mr. Eliot and Mr. Murry. But the problem of the relation of poetry to thought is very difficult. ' The relation of poetic diction to poetic thought', Mr. Herbert Read writes (*Phases of English Poetry*, 1928, p. 50), ' is a comparatively unexplored subject; I am not sure that there is any necessary connection between them at all. His diction makes or mars the poet; it is the expression of his sensibility, and as such is unequivocal. The thought of a poet is a factor which will enhance his general " value ", but it does not alter his poetic value.' I take Mr. Read to mean by 'his general " value " ' the poet's value, as e.g. a philosopher or painter *plus* his poetic value. But I am not sure he is not going too far. A poet's sensibility *is* partly a matter of his beliefs. Wordsworth's poetry would be different from what it is, though not necessarily either better or worse, if he had been a Roman Catholic. The real point, I believe, is that it is never (to borrow a phrase from Mr. I. A. Richards) ' what a poem *says* that matters, but what it *is* '. A poet's thoughts and beliefs are one of the elements that go to make up his poem, but once incorporated in it they lose their specific character and become a part, an aspect, of the intellectual and emotional complex that is the poem. A sort of pantheism *can* be extracted from Wordsworth's ' Tintern Abbey ', but the thing extracted is very different in isolation, gasping on the bank, from what it is in the poem. There it is dead; in the poem it is alive precisely because it is not detachable. The poetic justification of an idea or belief is simply that it shall provide an integral part in the complete organism of the poem. The idea or belief that meets this requirement is a poetic asset; the idea or belief that fails to

Professor Frye's theory (it is not only his but is very generally held in America) is thus open to exactly the same objection as the sociological theory of Leslie Stephen. They are both attempts to interpret the course of literary evolution in terms of something irrelevant to literature. It may be said that they *work*, but on examination they will be found to be only tolerable in proportion to the impurity of the works of literature with which they deal. They possess a certain plausibility in the fields of the drama and the novel. But the drama and the novel are relatively impure forms of literature. Social conditions and 'ideas' are part of the material which they exploit, and inferior or careless dramatists and novelists have sometime sacrificed to them the essentially literary qualities of their works. It is in poetry, the purest of the literary forms, that the futility of these attempts becomes evident.

> Come away, come away, death,
>     And in sad cypress let me be laid;
> Fly away, fly away, breath;
>     I am slain by a fair cruel maid.

The literary historians are helpless when confronted with the lyrics of Shakespeare. What is their function in the social organism? Where are their universal ideas and principles? But theories of literary history which are compelled to pass by poetry only because it is perfect are self-condemned.

The failure of the existing theories of literary

meet it is a liability. But the test is not the value of the idea or belief in itself, *in vacuo*, but its congeniality or uncongeniality in the particular poem.

history has been due to the fact that their sponsors have not been interested so much in literature as in the extraneous matters that they have tried to read into literature. Literature can only be interpreted in terms of something essential to it. A theory of the history of literature must be based upon an understanding of the nature of literature. I propose to approach the problem by a reconsideration of the difference between poetry and prose.

## II

Poetry can be regarded (apart from metaphorical extensions of the word) as either the alternative or the antithesis to prose. It is a matter of emphasis. In one sense of the word—as when Milton describes poetry as 'simple, sensuous, and passionate'—the emphasis will be on the qualities that it shares with prose. (In this sense the word is roughly equivalent to 'imaginative literature'.) But the emphasis can also be on the qualities that differentiate poetry from prose, the technical differences between two distinct and opposed modes of expression. And it is this last sense of the word that alone concerns us here. For poetry in the sense of an alternative to prose appeals primarily by its matter—the difference in *matter* between an epitaph and an obituary notice is often negligible; whereas the primary appeal of poetry in the sense of the antithesis to prose is by its manner. And to the literary historian it is the manner, not the matter, that counts, the technique and not the theme, the virtuosity and not the philosophy.

Coleridge was, of course, speaking of poetry in the antithetical sense of the word when he defined it as 'the best words in the best order'. The definition does not go far, but it has one merit at any rate—that of excluding irrelevant considerations. For the critical difference between the words, taken as one element, and every other conceivable constituent of a poem is this: The words make the poem; other qualities can only add to it. A poem without words is not a poem at all; whereas a poem without simplicity (such as Donne's 'Anatomy'), or without sensuousness (such as Pope's 'Essay on Man'), or without passion (such as Keats's 'Fancy'), if possibly not easy or exciting or profound, does not cease *ipso facto* to be poetry.

But Coleridge's definition deserves to be quoted in its entirety. It exists in two forms. The first, which is the more familiar, runs as follows: 'I wish our clever young poets would remember my homely definitions of prose and poetry; that is, prose = words in their best order;—poetry = the *best* words in the best order.'[1] The second is fuller and more explicit:

The definition of good Prose is—proper words in their proper places;—of good Verse—the most proper words in their proper places. The propriety is in either case relative. The words in prose ought to express the intended meaning, and no more; if they attract attention to themselves, it is, in general, a fault. In the very best styles, as Southey's, you read page after page, understanding the author perfectly, without once taking notice of the medium of communication;

[1] *Specimens of the Table-Talk*, vol. i, 1835, p. 84.

—it is as if he had been speaking to you all the while. But in verse you must do more;—there the words, the *media*, must be beautiful, and ought to attract your notice—yet not so much and so perpetually as to destroy the unity which ought to result from the whole poem.[1]

The question that Coleridge's definition immediately raises is this: If words are the *media* of poetry, what are the *media* of prose? And the answer would seem to be, Ideas. 'In prose', as Whately once pointed out, 'the language is the vehicle for the matter; in poetry, the matter is the vehicle for the language.'[2] In prose, that is, the words tend to be submerged in the ideas or things they represent. One synonym is as good as another. In poetry, on the other hand, the words are always liable to interfere with, and even in extreme cases to contradict, the theme or argument. 'Pure' prose is entirely a matter of ideas; 'pure' poetry is entirely a matter of phrases. It is for this reason that prose is more easily translated than poetry. An idea, being independent of the words in which it is expressed, can move from one language into another without inconvenience. But a phrase will not travel. A phrase is a collection of words, and its virtue lies in the words being just the words they are, with just the sounds and associations that they happen to possess and that their equivalents in foreign languages generally do not. What it comes to is that words are double-sided. They possess both a denotation and a connotation. One side of a word, the side

---

[1] *Specimens of the Table-Talk*, vol. ii, p. 214.
[2] *Miscellaneous Remains*, 1864, p. 137.

that prose seizes upon, is to all intents and purposes simply a label, which can be affixed or detached without affecting the word itself at all. This is a word's denotation. The other side, the connotation of a word, is more stable, less arbitrary, because it is primarily a matter of the word's sound, which is constant, and secondarily of the associations with other words that the sound imposes. And it is this side, though not to the exclusion of the other (except perhaps in the experiments of Mallarmé and his followers), that poetry exploits.

But the point of real interest—a point evaded by Coleridge—is not the differences between poetry and prose but the reason for those differences. Why are words the *media* of poetry and ideas of prose? Why does poetry employ both the connotations and the denotations of words when prose is restricted to their denotations? The explanation, I believe, lies in the difference between the nature of the prosaic and the poetic statement.[1]

Prose is essentially, as the etymology of the word suggests, a mode of progression. A novel and a treatise both take you from one point to another. When you have reached the last chapter you have got to something quite different from that with which you started in the first chapter. A poem, on the other hand, stands still. The reading of a poem, instead of being, like the reading of a novel, a series of related experiences, is a single and distinct

---

[1] This is, of course, only to carry the investigation a step farther. The ultimate origins of poetry and prose are probably to be found in the memory and the ratiocinative faculty respectively.

experience to which each of the phrases contributes something. Prose progresses gradually and cumulatively through a continuous series of propositions, the attention concentrating in turn on the different stages in the development of the narrative or argument, and, except for its immediate relevance, either forgetting or relegating to the memory what came before. Poetry, however, overriding the intermediate connexions of grammar, tends to fuse its separate and scattered statements into a complicated and instantaneous whole. It is 'esemplastic', to use Coleridge's word. The parts of a poem, that is, must be read against a background of awareness of the whole. The attention therefore, instead of being concentrated as in prose, is diffused, referring both backwards and forwards as it collects the scattered implications of words and images.

> In the poetic period not only the attribute, but every word, every moment of thought, gathers up, renews the whole. The subject is recalled in its concept in every word of the proposition.[1]

The number of points that can be contained in the vision at the same time is not absolutely limited and can be increased. It is the same, to some extent, with the inner eye of the consciousness. An almost infinite number of statements can be presented before it at the same time. But they are not really instantaneous. What happens is that the attention is only directed towards one statement at a time, or rather one aspect only of a statement. They pass in succession across the field of consciousness, hovering and disappearing—only to reappear again with a rapidity that

[1] Leone Vivante, *Notes on the Originality of Thought*, 1927, p. 164.]

the imagination cannot grasp and that is equivalent, for us, to immobility. The poetic faculty consists in a superior degree of agility. It relaxes its hold upon a statement and then returns to it; it is at one point and it is everywhere; it is in the present and it is in the past. This relative *instantaneity* of the images in the perception is the essential factor in the act of poetic thought.[1]

A powerfully imaginative mind seizes and combines at the same instant all the important ideas of its poem or picture, and while it works with one of them, it is at the same instant working with and modifying all in their relation to it and never losing sight of their bearings on each other—as the motion of a snake's body goes through all parts at once and its volition acts at the same instant in coils which go contrary ways.[2]

But, when we have defined the prosaic statement as a link in a progressive series and the poetic statement as a part of an instantaneous whole, the further question meets us, How is it that the same words can behave so differently in poetry and in prose? Why are the words of prose progressive and the words of poetry stationary? A definition of the nature of poetic and prosaic statements is incomplete without an analysis of their structure.

The structure of prose is, in the widest sense of the word, *logical*; its statements are always ultimately reducible to a syllogistic form. A passage of prose, *any* passage, not even excluding so-called 'poetic' prose, resolves itself under analysis into a series of explanations, definitions, and conclusions. It is by

[1] I have translated these sentences from the Swedish writer Hans Larsson.

[2] T. E. Hulme, *Speculations*, 1924, pp. 139-40.

these means that the book progresses. They are the framework into which the content of prose—its subject-matter—must somehow or other be fitted :

Captain Wentworth had no fortune. He had been lucky in his profession, but spending freely what had come freely had realized nothing. But he was confident that he should soon be rich ; full of life and ardour he knew that he should soon have a ship and soon be on a station that would lead to everything he wanted. He had always been lucky ; he knew that he should be so still. Such confidence, powerful in its own warmth and bewitching in the wit which often expressed it, must have been enough for Anne ; but Lady Russell saw it very differently. His sanguine temper and fearlessness of mind operated very differently on her. She saw in it but an aggravation of the evil. It only added a dangerous character to himself. He was brilliant, he was headstrong ; Lady Russell had little taste for wit and of anything approaching to imprudence a horror. She deprecated the connexion in every light.[1]

(The statement that Captain Wentworth had no fortune is followed by a *definition* of ' no fortune '. He had had money but had spent it. The *explanation* of his having had money was that he had been lucky ; and it was *because* he had been lucky that he expected his luck to continue. His self-confidence was the *reason* that made Anne agree and Lady Russell disagree with him. The latter *concluded* that the connexion was undesirable.)

The structure of poetry, on the other hand, is ultimately determined by its technique. The part, that is, that is played by logic in prose falls in poetry to the metre, the rhymes, the alliterations, and the

[1] Jane Austen, *Persuasion*, ch. iv.

associative values of the words. For these devices, far from being merely decorative (as is sometimes suggested), are, when properly used, the *sine qua non* of poetry. Their function, indeed, is both negative and positive. Negatively, they repel the logical and progressive tendencies that are always active in speech. Positively, they hold the poem together by connecting up the separate phrases and stanzas and so ensuring the unity of a single and instantaneous whole.

A few examples are subjoined as guarantees of the plausibility of this contention.

(1) Between the loud stream and the trembling stars. (*Tennyson.*)

It will be observed that 'trembling stars' repeats five of the consonants (*l, s, t, r, m*) of 'loud stream'. What is the point of the alliteration? It was introduced, I believe, to bridge the apparent logical interval between the two images. The alliteration, by providing a connexion of sound, assists the reader to discern the poet's connexion of sense.

(2) The expense of spirit in a waste of shame. (*Shakespeare.*)

The line contains two submerged puns. 'Expense' suggests 'expanse' and prepares the way for 'waste'; 'waste' suggests 'waist', which reinforces the sexual implications of the sonnet.

(3) Mr. T. S. Eliot's 'Burbank with a Baedeker' contains the following lines:

> Her shuttered barge
> Burned on the water all the day.

And later :

> the God Hercules
> Had left him, that had loved him well.

Mr. Eliot is referring to two passages in *Antony and Cleopatra*,

> The barge she sat in, like a burnished throne
> Burned on the water ;

and

> 'Tis the god Hercules, whom Antony lov'd,
> Now leaves him.

The quotations provide the poem, which is otherwise incoherent, with a sort of subterranean framework. The dramatis personae, Burbank, Princess Volupine, and the Jews (Bleistein and Klein), become immediately intelligible when it is seen that Burbank is Antony, the Princess Cleopatra, and the Jews Caesar. The poem, in its sub-intention, is a modern sarcastic version of Shakespeare's play, but in Mr. Eliot's hands Cleopatra actually packs cards with Caesar, and Antony is left to commit intellectual suicide in the pages of his Baedeker.

> (4) But death shall lead her to a shade,
>    Where love is cold and beauty blind.   (*Davenant*.)

The second line contains a hypallage. For the point of the poem is not that beauty is *blind* in the grave but that it is *unseen*. The prose order would be 'Where love is blind and beauty cold'; the poetic order, instead of allowing the two images to fall apart, runs them together and produces a complicated image of very much richer content.[1]

---

[1] The examples given have been chosen to illustrate the four types

If these conclusions should be accepted, the explanation of the relative inconspicuousness of the words of good prose and the relative prominence of the words of good poetry will at once be apparent. The words of prose are inconspicuous because they form part of a logical structure. They are counters, representing like counters of another kind so much 'purchasing power', and, as they exist only to be exchanged, their services are necessarily temporary. The act of changing your twelve pennies into a shilling's worth of goods, or your premises into a conclusion, by terminating your connexion with the individual pennies and premises, destroys them for you. You retain what they represented, but under a new symbol. And so a word in prose has no value in itself. Its sphere of usefulness is limited to the relations, ultimately fatal to itself, that it establishes with other words. The result is that it becomes, as it were, transparent ; the meaning is seen through it, and the word itself, the symbol as distinct from the thing symbolized, is unnoticed.

The words of poetry are more conspicuous, more *solid*, because they are part of a structure which they themselves create. The principal words in a poem, by falling into the accented positions in the line, by rhyming, by alliterating, by connoting more than

---

under which the technical devices of poetry can all be subsumed. A codification, a sort of elementary poetic grammar, would be possible as follows : (*a*) repetitions of sound (rhythm, metre, rhyme, assonance, alliteration) ; (*b*) repetitions of sense (refrains, puns, ' ambiguities ') ; (*c*) repetitions of context (quotations, the use of proper names or specialized words from a particular literary tradition); (*d*) variations of the prose order (hypallages, inversions, zeugmas).

they denote, *call attention to themselves*. And so a reader of poetry is aware of the more important words he is reading in a way the reader of prose is not. The words are thrust upon his notice. The success of the words in obtruding themselves upon the reader—his consciousness of the *whole* word, its sound as well as its meaning, its past history and its present function—is the test of the poem's success. It is only by observing the words that the reader can become aware of the poem's structure; and it is only by an awareness of its structure that he can appreciate that unity and instantaneity that are the hallmarks of the perfect poem.[1]

## III

The main lines of the theory of literary history which I wish to propound, at any rate as it concerns poetry, will by this time be evident.

A history of poetry, which is to be something more than a series of critical essays, is only conceivable, as we have seen, in terms of something essential to poetry. That was my first point. But poetry, reduced to its simplest terms, is nothing more than a mode of expression the *media* of which

---

[1] I am not a philosopher and this brief summary of an intricate subject should not be mistaken for a contribution to aesthetics. The reader who is in search of a more professional discussion of the differences between poetry and prose may be referred to Professor Alexander's *Beauty and Other Forms of Value* (1933). Professor Alexander, however, equates poetry with drama, whereas I hold that drama, including poetic drama, is essentially a form of prose because its *media* are not words but ideas —especially, of course, those ideas that come under the heading of 'character in action'. The fact that plays can often be translated with little or no loss would seem to bear out my contention.

are words. That was my second point. It is to words therefore, their history and science, that I invite the historian of poetry to turn. I suggest that poetry develops *pari passu* with the words it uses, that its history is a part of the general history of language, and that its changes of style and mood are merely the reflection of changing tendencies in the uses to which language is being put.[1]

In the following pages I shall attempt to test the possibilities of this theory by an examination of the main stream of English poetry, from the Renaissance to the present day, in the light of the semantic history of the English language. They should not be mistaken, however, for a full-dress history of English poetry. They are rather, in the eighteenth-century sense of the word, *proposals* for the more ambitious work I hope one day to write.

[1] Including, of course, the social and ethical influences stressed by Leslie Stephen and Professor Frye. But my point is that these influences reach the poets at second hand. Their immediate impact is not with poetry (which is immune from infection by its nature) but with language. That is the way languages change. A dominant influence will leave its imprint not only on a few favourite words but on the manner in which *all* words are used. But a linguistic change, though it may cause a poetic change, is not identical with it. A patriot of the school of Freeman and Furnivall may perhaps induce us to call a preface a ' foreword '; he can never, simply by virtue of his patriotism, impose a new poetic manner on us. Indirectly, however, the patriots *may* influence the poets. For, if they can only get enough words like ' foreword ' adopted into the language, its *direction* will be affected ; and change of linguistic direction seems always to involve a change of poetic style.

## II
## ELIZABETHANS, METAPHYSICALS, AUGUSTANS

THE history of poetry is, in one sense, the history of the *criticism* of poetry. For it is the critic who creates the *data* that the historian must clarify and co-ordinate, and in the absence of such criticism the historian is reduced, unless he is his own critic (a hazardous combination), to the humbler role of bibliographer. Moreover, the value of a history will depend upon the kind of criticism on which it is based, the best criticism, because the least irrelevant, being that of the poets themselves and the second best that of their contemporaries. It is for these reasons that a serious history of English poetry only becomes possible in the Elizabethan period. Of the earlier poetry almost no contemporary criticism has survived, and its place is inadequately taken, for the present purpose, by modern guess-work, however learned or enthusiastic.

## I

Elizabethan poetry begins with Wyatt and Surrey. It begins, that is, with the *Songes and Sonettes, written by the ryght honorable Lorde Henry Haward late Earle of Surrey, and other*, which is now known as Tottel's Miscellany. Elizabethan criticism is a month or so younger. Tottel's first edition was published on June the 5th, 1557 (rather more than a year before Elizabeth came to the throne); Sir John Cheke's

letter to Sir Thomas Hoby, which is not only the
first piece of Elizabethan criticism but almost the
first piece of literary criticism in the modern sense
of the word in English, was written on July the 16th
of the same year. But the coincidence is more than
one of date. Elizabethan poetry and Elizabethan
criticism were expressions of essentially the same
impulse. The poetry was a kind of criticism. They
were applications, one practical, one theoretical, of
a single attitude to literature—that of the craftsman.

Wyatt's and Surrey's position in the Elizabethan
hierarchy is analogous to Denham's and Waller's in
that of the Augustans. They were 'the first reformers of our English meetre and stile ',[1] 'the first
polishers of our vulgar Poesie ',[2] 'the first refiners
of the English tong '.[3] Their importance, in other
words, was primarily technical. They were innova-
tors and experimenters, and their legacy to the
Elizabethans was first of all a new point of view to
poetry, a new curiosity about questions of prosody
and style. The earlier English poetry, since Chaucer,
had been marked by a certain bland unselfconscious-
ness. At its best, as in Skelton, it had had a blithe
helter-skelter spontaneity ; but its norm was
mechanical and monotonous, a jog-trot. With Wyatt
and Surrey poetry became learned. It ceased to be
the haphazard creature of whim, a hit-or-miss affair,

---

[1] [Richard Puttenham ?], *The Arte of English Poesie*, 1589. Quotation from reprint in G. Gregory Smith, *Elizabethan Critical Essays*,
vol. ii, 1904, p. 63.                    [2] Ibid., p. 131.
[3] Sir John Harington, 'A Preface, or rather a Briefe Apologie of
Poetrie' (prefixed to *Orlando Furioso*, 1591). Quotation from Gregory
Smith, op. cit., vol. ii, p. 219.

and became amenable once again, or so it seemed, to a conscious and purposive control. The older poetry had written itself; the New Poetry, as it has been called, was a deliberate exercise in style, an attempt to create a special order of literary effects by means of conscious innovations of metre and diction.

The special relevance of the Elizabethan critics to Elizabethan poetry is that they reflect and clarify the problem that underlies these technical experiments. That problem, as we shall see, was one of language. The Elizabethans knew that from one cause and another—their closer relations with the Continent, the revival of learning, the invention of printing—something had *happened* to the English language. It was not the language their fathers had used; the old literary forms were no longer adequate to it. The importance of Cheke's letter to Hoby is that it introduces for the first time a theory of language that was directly complementary to Wyatt's and Surrey's practice. Hoby had translated Castiglione's *Cortegiano*, and Cheke, who had revised the manuscript, was writing to him to justify his emendations. (The letter was eventually published with the translation in 1561.) The crucial passage is Cheke's condemnation of Hoby's foreign words :

I am of this opinion that our own tung shold be written cleane and pure, unmixt and unmangeled with borowing of other tunges, wherein if we take not heed bi tiim, ever borowing and never payeng, she shall be fain to keep her house as bankrupt. For then doth our tung naturallie and praisablie utter her meaning, whan she bouroweth no counterfeitness of other tunges to attire her self withall, but useth plainlie her own, with such shift, as nature, craft, experiens and folowing of other excellent doth lead her unto, and if she want at ani tiim (as being unperfight she must) yet let her borow with suche bashfulnes, that it mai appeer, that if either the mould of our own tung could serve us to falcion a woord of our own, or if the old denisoned wordes could content and ease this neede, we wold not boldly venture of unknowen wordes.

The theory of language implied by Cheke, that of a flux, is the theory that lies, in a half-conscious and unformulated state, behind almost the whole of the poetry and criticism of the Elizabethans. The natural condition of language, in the absence of artificial restraints, seemed to them to be one of gradual corruption; a 'cleane and pure' tongue could only be obtained by a process of insulation. But Cheke's metaphor ('ever borowing and never payeng') was misleading. The metaphor that the later critics used was that of a stream. 'The ceaselesse flowing river of our tongue' is Chapman's image,[1] and it exactly defines the Elizabethan point of view. Their language seemed to be flowing away from them. Words were dropping out of use, new words were coming in, and meanings were changing all the time, 'extraordinary occasions, by little & little, as it were insensibly, bringing in of many corruptions that creep along with the time'.[2] And not unnaturally, as the powerlessness of reformers like Cheke became evident, a certain fatalism

[1] 'To the Understander' (prefixed to *Achilles Shield*, 1598). Quotation from Gregory Smith, op. cit., vol. ii, p. 305.

[2] Puttenham, op. cit. Quotation from Gregory Smith, op. cit., vol. ii, p. 149.

resulted. It has found memorable expression in a sentence in Daniel's *A Defence of Ryme* (1603). 'But this is but a Character of that perpetuall revolution which we see to be in all things that never remaine the same : and we must heerein be content to submit our selves to the law of time, which in few yeeres wil make al that for which we now contend Nothing.'[1] The disintegrating forces in language seemed to be too strong to be resisted.

The theory of a linguistic flux is not confined to the Elizabethans. It is implied in Horace's *Ars Poetica*, and Pope adopted it—with half an eye perhaps on the passage in Horace :

> Our sons their fathers' failing language see,
> And such as Chaucer is, shall Dryden be.[2]

But there is a difference between this attitude and that of the Elizabethans. In Horace and Pope the theory is invoked to provide an elegant rhetorical effect. The lines are only half-serious. But the Elizabethans were entirely serious. The theory was the inevitable projection of their practice. The fluid and diffuse style that represents the main current of Elizabethan poetry—it runs from Surrey through Spenser to Drayton—*demanded* a theory of flux to explain and justify it. The theory was implied by the style. Their common origin was a misunderstanding, as it proved, of the nature of sixteenth-century English. The Renaissance and the Reformation had stimulated and widened the country's

---

[1] Quotation from Gregory Smith, op. cit., vol. ii, p. 383.
[2] *An Essay of Criticism.*

curiosity, and writers, finding the old vocabulary no longer adequate to their new interests, were compelled to borrow words from foreign languages and to extend the meaning of those already in use. Exact statistics are not available, but it seems probable that the language almost *doubled* itself in the course of the century.[1] But the procedure, natural and even admirable though it was, was viewed by the critics with the blankest consternation. Cheke's verdict has already been quoted. It was the first of a series of warnings—'our English tongue,' E. K. complained (speaking for Spenser), was 'a gallimaufray or hodgepodge of al other speches'[2]—that culminate in Bacon's gloomy dictum that 'these modern languages will at one time or other play the bankrupt with books'.[3]

And this mood of linguistic suspicion was shared by the poets. The style they adopted was designed, it would seem, to *counterbalance* the tendencies of the language. They had an uneasy feeling all the time that their vocabulary was slipping away from under them, and, suspecting and distrusting it, they did not dare to confide the whole of their meaning to a single word or phrase. (That word or phrase might be obsolete before the year was out.) And so they reinforced their primary meanings with

[1] An analysis of 40 pages of the *Shorter Oxford Dictionary* has shown that of every 100 words in use in 1600, 39 were introduced between 1500 and 1600.

[2] Dedication prefixed to *The Shepheardes Calender*, 1579.

[3] Letter to Sir Tobie Matthew, 1623, quoted by J. L. Moore, *Tudor-Stuart Views on the Growth, Status and Destiny of the English Language* 1910, p. 8.

repetitions, glosses, and amplifications. A shower
of words and images splashes the reader's face :

> Thrise happie she, that is so wel assured
>    Unto her selfe and setled so in hart :
>    that nether will for better be allured,
>    ne feard with worse to any chaunce to start :
> But like a steddy ship doth strongly part
>    the raging waves and keepes her course aright :
>    ne ought for tempest doth from it depart,
>    ne ought for fayrer weathers false delight.
> Such selfe assurance need not feare the spight
>    of grudging foes, ne favour seek of friends :
>    but in the stay of her owne stedfast might,
>    nether to one her selfe nor other bends.
> Most happy she that most assured doth rest,
>    but he most happy who such one loves best.

Spenser's sonnet (No. LIX of the *Amoretti*) is
typical, in its diffuseness and repetitions, of the
Elizabethan style. His lady is not only *well assured*
but *settled in heart*; the ship to which she is compared is both *steady* and *keeps her course*. And the
antithetical alternatives are presented with a merci-
less fullness. The lady is neither *allured for better* nor
*feared with worse*, and, impervious equally to *tempest*
and *fairer weather*, she need not *fear the spite of foes*
or *seek the favour of friends*. The later critics called
this 'copie', a word that was intended to represent
the Latin *copia verborum*. Bacon contrasts it with
'weight'—'the whole inclination and bent of those
times [the Renaissance] was rather towards copie
than weight'.[1] It is a quality rather out of favour

[1] *The Twoo Bookes of the Proficience and Advancement of Learning,*

to-day; we are too near to the 'copie' of the Victorians. But its limitations were recognized even then, and we find Jonson complaining that 'Now because they speake all they can how ever unfitly they are thought to have the greater copy'.[1] There is, indeed, a disconcerting flatness and lack of emphasis in the facile, fluent style of the Elizabethans. The non-committal tautologies result in a verbal smudge; the meaning is so diffused that it escapes. An Elizabethan poet distrusted language —in a last resort he would always rather have written his poems without words. Gascoigne actually recommended the aspiring writer to ground his poem 'upon some fine invention. For, that beyng founde, pleasant woordes will follow well inough and fast inough'.[2]

It is permissible to regret the diffuseness of Elizabethan poetry. But our regrets should not blind us to the fact that, the English language being what it then was, a degree of poetic diffuseness was inevitable. Poetry is not made out of the words in dictionaries, but the words we meet on the lips and in the writings of our contemporaries. The words an Elizabethan poet met were, to a degree it is

1605. Quotation from selection in J. E. Spingarn, *Critical Essays of the Seventeenth Century*, vol. i, 1908, p. 3.

[1] *Timber, or Discoveries* (written 1620–35?). Quotation from selection in Spingarn, op. cit., vol. i, p. 22.

[2] *Certayne Notes of Instruction*, 1575. Quotation from Gregory Smith's reprint, op. cit., vol. i, p. 47. Gascoigne was writing as a professional. The academic point of view is represented by Ascham's caveat (*The Scholemaster*, 1570; reprinted Gregory Smith, op. cit., vol. i, p. 6): 'Ye know not what hurt ye do to learning, that care not for wordes but for matter, and so make a devorse betwixt the tong and the hart.'

difficult to realize now, words that were new and strange to him, and often only half-understood and half-remembered. It should not surprise us therefore if the words of the Elizabethan poets sometimes seem to have less than their ordinary meaning. A new word is necessarily imprecise ; it has only half the meaning of an old-established word. The diffuseness of Elizabethan poetry was imposed on the poets willy-nilly by the high proportion of new or partially assimilated words they were compelled to use. And they were without the compensations their successors possessed. A new word, if it is less precise than an old word, may be expected to make up in glamour what it lacks in precision. There can be something very dashing and engaging about a brand-new word. But sixteenth-century English, particularly the English of the first three quarters of the century, was far from being dashing. Its temper is apologetic and embarrassed, uncertain of itself and despairing of its future, and the loan-words and neologisms, because of their number, instead of acting as stimulants to the language only decreased its self-confidence. The omens were not propitious for poetry.

## II

The theory of language as flux was superseded, by a natural transition, by a theory of language as progress. The stream of the Elizabethans' metaphor obtained a direction ; it was not merely flowing, it was flowing *somewhere*.

The turning-point is in or about 1590. At this period a new respect for the English language,

rising in some cases to a perfervid enthusiasm, begins to make itself heard.[1] (The new nationalism
that had come to a head with the defeat of the
Armada was probably a contributory cause.) Chapman's undertaking, in 1598, to prove his ' mother
tongue above all others for Poesie '[2] is typical of
the change, as is Florio's eulogy, also in 1598, of
' the copie and varietie of our sweete-mother-toong,
which under this most Excellent Princesse is growne
farre beyond that of former times '.[3] (These utter-
ances may be contrasted with William Webbe's
query, only twelve years earlier, ' What shoulde be
the cause that our English speeche, in some of the
wysest mens judgements, hath never attained to
anie sufficient ripenes ? '.[4]) But the most elaborate
example of this mood of self-confidence is Richard
Carew's *Epistle on the Excellency of the English Tongue.*
The thesis of Carew's essay—written in emulation of Henri Estienne's *Projet du livre intitulé :
de la Précellence du langage françois,* and composed
either in 1595 or 1596, though not published until
1614—is reasonable enough—' that our English
Langwadge for all or the most is macheable, if not

---

[1] ' The earlier critics have an uneasy sense of the imperfections of
English. Leaving aside Tyndale's perfervid defence of its sufficiency
for Bible-translating (1528), in which More agreed with him, we have
up to the year 1561 blame, from 1561 to the end of the century blame
and praise commingled, . . . throughout the whole of the seventeenth
century nothing but praise.' J. L. Moore, op. cit., p. 15.

[2] ' To the Reader ' (prefixed to *Seaven Bookes of the Iliades of Homere,*
1598). Quotation from Gregory Smith's reprint, op. cit., vol. ii, p. 297.

[3] ' The Epistle Dedicatorie ' (prefixed to *A Worlde of Wordes,* 1598).

[4] *A Discourse of English Poetrie,* 1586. Quotation from Gregory
Smith's reprint, op. cit., vol. i, p. 227.

preferable, before any other in vogue at this daye '.[1]
But the tone becomes more extravagant as the argument progresses, and Carew roundly concludes
'that the most renowned of other nations have
laied up, as in Treasure, and entrusted the *Divisos
orbe Britannos* with the rarest Jewelles of their lipps
perfections, whether yow respect the understanding
for significancye, or the memorye for Easynes, or
the conceipt for plentifullness, or the Eare for
pleasauntnes '.[2] The really interesting thing, however, about Carew is not his superlatives, but his
candid recognition of the fact that the loan-words
and 'inkhornisms' which had so frightened the
Elizabethans were bracing and enriching the language. English had proved itself. The first alarms
that it might be swamped in the flood of new and
foreign words had turned out to be unnecessary.
The language had incorporated the new-comers
without compromising its individuality, and it came
to be seen that the receptiveness of English, far
from being a weakness, was a principal source of
its strength. Sorbières, a French visitor, described
the English as being 'great Admirers of their own
Language. It must needs be very Copious and
Adapt, for it openly declares it to be her Business
to grow Rich with the Spoils of all dead Languages,
and every Day impunedly to appropriate all that is
good and proper for her from the living ones.'[3]

---

[1] Edited in Gregory Smith, op. cit., vol. ii, p. 286.
[2] Ibid., pp. 293–4.
[3] *A Voyage to England. Done into English from the French Original*,
1709, p. 70. The French edition appeared in 1664.

Sorbières wrote shortly after the Restoration, but his words would have been just as true if they had been written sixty years earlier. ' For the first quality ', Mr. George Gordon has noted, ' of Eliza-bethan, and therefore of Shakespearian English, is its power of hospitality, its passion for free experi-ment, its willingness to use every form of verbal wealth, to try anything.' [1] It was a habit of mind that sometimes took strange forms. The anony-mous author of *The First Booke of the Preservation of King Henry the VII* (1599) is to be found justifying his clumsy hexameters on the ground that they ' will enrich our speach with good and significant wordes '.[2] And Miles Smith, in the preface to the Authorized Version of the Bible, makes the curious boast that several English words had been used to translate one Greek or Hebrew word, 'lest they should seem to wrong the copious English tongue '.[3]

But these eccentricities were part of an entirely serious and rational movement. A new attitude to language had come into being. The restrictive and isolationist doctrines of the earlier period had been discarded in favour of an expansionist policy of freedom and plunder. And with the changed point of view there came a change of linguistic theory. Language was no longer thought of as something inorganic—a flowing river or a bankrupt business. It had come to life. The English tongue was an infant giant, who was growing stronger and bolder

[1] *Shakespeare's English*, S.P.E., 1928, p. 259.
[2] Reprinted in Gregory Smith, op. cit., vol. i, p. 378.
[3] Quoted by J. L. Moore, op. cit., p. 32.

every year, and the introduction of neologisms and foreign and classical loan-words was a natural tribute to the voracity of his young appetite. The emphasis, that is, was on the language's growth. The increases in the vocabulary were a qualitative as well as a quantitative gain. English was better because it was bigger. A rudimentary theory of progress was therefore implied.[1]

And this organic conception of language ran parallel to an organic conception of literature. The feature that the later Elizabethan and the Jacobean critics single out in the writings of their contemporaries is precisely its vitality, its 'life'. 'And for his Poësie,' Horace says of Virgil in Jonson's *Poetaster* (acted 1601),

> 'tis so ramm'd with Life,
> That it shall gather strength of Life with being,
> And live hereafter, more admir'd then now.[2]

The word was a favourite of Jonson's. 'How shall you looke for wit', he demands in *Discoveries*, 'from him whose leasure and head yeeld you no life or sharpenesse in his writing?'[3] And Bolton praises the 'vital, judicious, and most practicable Language' of Jonson's own poems.[4] The theory of style that

---

[1] The theory occasionally becomes explicit. Fleckno, for example (*Miscellania*, 1653, p. 104), writing of the state of affairs before 1642, speaks of 'the perfectioning of our Language towards which it was advancing amain'.

[2] Quotation from Gregory Smith's reprint of selections, op. cit., vol. ii, p. 395.

[3] Quotation from selection reprinted in Spingarn, op. cit., vol. i, p. 44.

[4] *Hypercritica: or A Rule of Judgment, for writing or reading our History's* [1618 ?]. Quotation from Spingarn's reprint, op. cit., vol. i, p. 111.

these judgements imply is Buffon's : *Le style, c'est l'homme.* For the test of a style's vitality is that it shall reflect the idiosyncrasies of its author. 'That which we thinke', said Nashe, 'let us speake, and that which we speake let us thinke ; let our speeche accorde with our life.'[1] 'There be', said Putten-ham, 'that have called stile the image of man, *mentis character* ; for man is but his minde, and as his minde is tempered and qualified, so are his speeches and language at large, and his inward con-ceits be the mettall of his minde, and his manner of utterance the very warp & woofe of his conceits.'[2] '*Oratio imago animi*,' said Jonson, 'Language most shewes a man : speake, that I may see thee.'[3]

The theories of language as organism, of poetry as 'life', and of style as the man, were complemen-tary—the one implied the others. And their com-bination resulted in a consistent and workmanlike aesthetic. But there is one objection that this aes-thetic invites. A style that is the man must tend to produce, together with the qualities the author shares with others, qualities that are peculiar to him. It may degenerate, in an extreme instance, into a kind of private language. A degree of obscurity therefore was the necessary concomitant of the un-rivalled *sincerity* of the metaphysical style. It was the defect of its quality. It can be defended because it was inevitable. 'Obscurity in affection of words',

---

[1] *The Anatomie of Absurdities*, 1589. Quotation from Gregory Smith's reprint, op. cit., vol. i, p. 335.

[2] Op. cit., p. 154.

[3] *Timber, or Discoveries.* Quotation from Spingarn's selection, op. cit., vol. i, p. 41.

Chapman pointed out, ' and indigested conceits, is
pedantical and childish ; but when it shroudeth itself in the heart of his subject, uttered with fitness
of figure and expressive epithets, with that darkness
will I still labour to be shadowed.'[1] The distinction was a relevant one. For the essential obscurity
is often more apparent than real. There *are* lines
in Chapman and in Donne that are almost unintelligible out of their context. But restore these lines
to the poem they come from and read them with
something of the concentration with which they
were written, and the difficulties disappear almost
at once. Coleridge, indeed, in a paradoxical mood,
once maintained that the pre-Restoration writers
were more lucid than the Augustans. ' In them ',
he said, ' the precise intended meaning of a word
can never be mistaken ; whereas in the latter
writers, as especially in Pope, the use of words is
for the most part purely arbitrary, so that the context will rarely show the true specific sense, but
only that something of the sort is designed.'[2]    But
no one but Coleridge would have thought of praising the metaphysical style for its lucidity. It is the
range and subtlety of their language that the contemporary critics seized upon. ' Where have you ',
Fleckno inquired, ' for that which we call Rhetor-
icke, Eloquence, and high expression, a Language
excelling ours ? or that speakes more by Figure
and Metaphor (the mayne ornaments of speech,
and the subtility of a Language) he being sayd to

[1] 'Preface' (to *Ovid's Banquet of Sence*, 1595).
[2] 'On Style' (in *Essays and Lectures*).

speak simply, whose words infold not a double
sense and meaning ? ' [1]

The suggestion of disparagement with which
Fleckno refers to those who ' speak simply ' cannot
be missed. Obviously he preferred ' a double sense
and meaning '. And as it happens ' a double sense ',
or ambiguity, is one of the most characteristic
features of the metaphysical style. Mr. William
Empson's *Seven Types of Ambiguity*, an elaborate
study of this poetic device, derives the majority of its
examples, and certainly the most telling ones, from
the poetry of this period.[2] The device runs right

---

[1] *Miscellania*, 1653, p. 102.

[2] An example missed by Mr. Empson is George Herbert's 'The Sonne':

> Let forrain nations of their language boast
> What fine varietie each tongue affords ;
> I like our language, as our men and coast,
> Who cannot dresse it well, want wit, not words.

And the feature that Herbert admired most in English was its
homonyms :

> How neatly do we give one onely name
> To parents' issue and the sunne's bright starre!

Herbert's ' Even-Song ' contains an application of this ' neat ' ambiguity :

> But much more blest be God above,
> Who gave me sight alone,
> Which to Himself He did denie :
> For when He sees my waies, I die ;
> But I have got His Sonne, and He hath none.

Richard Carew (*Epistle on the Excellency of the English Tongue*, ed.
Gregory Smith, op. cit., vol. ii, p. 288) displays the same enthusiasm
when contemplating the homonyms in English: ' Yea, soe significant are
our wordes, that amongst them sundry single ones serve to expresse
divers things ; as by *Bill* are ment a weapon, a scroll, and a birdes
beake ; by *Grave*, sober, a tombe, and to carve ; and by *light, marcke,
match, file, sore & praye*, the semblable.' Charles Cooper, on the other
hand, who represents later seventeenth-century opinion, praises English

through the Jacobean and Caroline poets. It is to be found even in such a simple-seeming writer as Herrick:

> A sweet disorder in the dresse
> Kindles in cloathes a wantonnesse :
> A Lawne about the shoulders thrown
> Into a fine distraction :
> An erring Lace, which here and there
> Enthralls the Crimson Stomacher :
> A Cuffe neglectfull, and thereby
> Ribbands to flow confusedly :
> A winning wave (deserving Note)
> In the tempestuous petticote :
> A carelesse shooe-string, in whose tye
> I see a wilde civility :
> Doe more bewitch me, then when Art
> Is too precise in every part.

The impression of a surprising richness, and almost grandeur (as of a painting by Titian), with a certain tantalizing quality, that Herrick's poem leaves, is primarily due to the skill with which he has exploited the ambiguous associations of the epithets. On the surface his subject is the 'Delight in Disorder' of the title—a disorder, that is, of costume. But a second subject is hinted at, though not protruded : a delight in disorder, not of costume but of manners and morals. It is not only the clothes but their wearers too whom he would have *sweet, wanton, distracted, erring, neglectful, winning, tempestuous, wild,* and *bewitching* rather than *precise.* The poem, in fact, instead of being the mere *jeu d'esprit* that it

for its freedom from the homonyms that disfigure Latin (*Grammatica Anglicana,* 1685, quoted by J. L. Moore, op. cit., p. 21).

would seem to be, is essentially a plea for paganism. There are three themes : (1) untidiness is becoming; (2) the clothes are the woman; (3) anti-Puritanism. But the success of the poem depends upon the fact that the themes are not isolated and contrasted but grow out of and into each other. The suspension between the various meanings produces a range of reference that none of them would have alone.

The condition of the English language in the first half of the seventeenth century was especially favourable to poetic ambiguities. A language, considered semantically, evolves by a series of conflicts between the denotative and the connotative forces in words—between 'an asceticism tending to kill language by stripping words of all association and a hedonism tending to kill language by dissipating their sense under a multiplicity of associations'.[1] The seventeenth century in England, from this point of view, was predominantly a connotative period. It was an epoch, linguistically as well as politically, of expansion. New words were being coined or borrowed all the time, and the tendencies that made for the introduction of new words were also active in adding new shades of meaning and new areas of context (a breeding-ground for the poetic ambiguity) in words already in use. (Thomas Carew actually associates 'the juggling feat of two-edged words' with 'whatsoever wrong By ours was done the Greek or Latin tongue'.[2]) The process

---

[1] *Oxford Poetry*, 1927.
[2] 'An Elegy upon the Death of Dr. Donne.'

was sometimes carried so far that the primary senses of words almost disappear in their derived meanings and associations. The phrases of Shakespeare and Donne, in particular, often seem to be on the point of sloughing their original meanings and vanishing, bright winged things, in the aura of suggestion they irradiate. Consider, for example, their use of the word *brave* :

> How beauteous mankind is ! O brave new world,
> That has such people in't.

> I have done one braver thing
>     Than all the Worthies did.

The word hovers between its normal meanings of 'courageous' and 'finely-dressed' and transcends them. Miranda's *new world* is not so much beautiful as exciting and romantic, a promised land of colour and adventure in which Right will always be Might ; and similarly Donne's *braver thing*—to 'forget the He and She '—is not essentially an act of courage but of grace, a chivalrous gesture of the Platonic knight. Herrick's ' Infanta ' is another and a more tangible example of the same process :

> Aske me why I send you here
>     This sweet Infanta of the yeere?

The dictionary defines ' Infanta ' as a 'daughter of the King and Queen of Spain or Portugal, especially the eldest daughter who is not heir to the throne'. That is what ' Infanta ' denotes. What it connotes, which was all Herrick was interested in, is an infant who is also an exotic princess. Herrick had no intention of *comparing* his primrose to the eldest

daughter of the King of Spain. That would be to
read a logical precision into his words that they do
not possess, and the possession of which would have
been fatal to the vague splendour of his poem.

The ambiguity and the use of words simply for
their associative values are particular instances of a
more general characteristic of the metaphysical style :
its tendency to push words a little beyond their
normal meanings. The peculiar vividness of metaphysical poetry is primarily due to the almost imperceptible twist—a ' perpetual slight alteration of
language, words perpetually juxtaposed in new and
sudden combinations, meanings perpetually *einge-
schachtelt* into meanings ' [1]—that by the unexpected
collocations of words and phrases it succeeded in
giving to language :

> Why does yon fellow falsify highways,
> And lays his life between the judge's lips
> To refine such a one ? Keeps horse and men
> To beat their valours for her ? [2]

> Let the priest in surplice white,
> That defunctive music can,
> Be the death-divining swan. [3]

*Falsify highways, beat their valours, defunctive music*—
such phrases are of the essence of metaphysical
poetry. They could only have been coined in these
sixty wonderful years, the Golden Age of English
poetry, between 1590 and 1650, and they were only
made possible by the peculiar vitality and elasticity

[1] T. S. Eliot, *The Sacred Wood*, 1920, p. 117.
[2] *The Revenger's Tragedy*, III. i.
[3] Shakespeare, ' The Phoenix and the Turtle '.

of the language of the period. But the device, for all its brilliant success, was fundamentally an abuse of language. A language is a vehicle of communication, or it is nothing. The metaphysical writers by continually extending the common meanings of words—the vividness they required was only obtainable so—gradually cut the ground away from under themselves. Their innovations, if they were to be innovations and not repetitions, had to be progressively more and more audacious and less and less intelligible. And it became impossible finally to say a plain thing in a plain way. The *impasse* is already evident in Shakespeare's *Henry VIII*:

> men might say,
> Till this time, pomp was single, but now married
> To one above itself.   Each following day
> Became the next day's master, till the last
> Made former wonders its.[1]

A style so tortuous and cumbrous, however capable it might be of momentary flashes of beauty, was no longer adequate as a medium of communication.

### III

Towards the middle of the seventeenth century the theory of language passed into a new phase. The theory of progress, which had displaced the earlier theory of flux, was superseded in its turn by a theory of cycles. Sir William Davenant was the first to define the new theory. 'Language', he wrote (in 1650), 'which is the onely Creature of Man's creation, hath like a Plant seasons of flourishing and

[1] I. i. 14–18.

decay, like Plants is remov'd from one soile to another, and by being so transplanted, doth often gather vigor and increase.'[1] The metaphor, it will be seen, is still that of an organism, but the emphasis has been transferred from the concept of growth to that of maturity. The metaphysicals had contemplated a continuous improvement of the language. It was to go on growing indefinitely. But as the century advanced it came to be seen that there must be a limit to this process of improvement. A language cannot go on growing for ever—it must in time grow up. 'Upon the whole', Leonard Welsted summed up, 'there is a Point of Perfection in general, which when once a Language is arriv'd to, it cannot exceed, tho' it may degenerate from it. . . . The vulgar Opinion therefore is a vulgar Error, *viz.* that our Language will continue to go on from one Refinement to another . . . till in Time the English, we now speak, is become as obsolete and unintelligible as that of Chaucer.'[2] (The 'vulgar Error', it is interesting to note, was the theory of progress of the earlier part of the century.)

Davenant's theory was an application to language of that cyclic theory of civilization which Sir William Temple popularized in England later in the century in his essay 'Of Ancient & Modern Learning'. The most succinct statement of it I have found is in Thomas Burnet's *Doctrina Antiqua* (1692). 'Not

---

[1] 'The Author's Preface' (in *Gondibert, An Heroick Poem*, 1650). Quotation from Spingarn's reprint, op. cit., vol. ii, p. 6.

[2] 'A Dissertation concerning the Perfection of the English Language, the State of Poetry, &c.' (prefixed to *Epistles, Odes, &c.*, 1724, p. ix).

only are Empires changed,' Burnet writes, ' but Learning, Manners and Religion, pass from one Country to another; and since all cannot enjoy them together, we do it alternately. Human Affairs are so ordered, as if it were decreed, that in such a Circle of Time, every Country and Nation should take its Turn, both in good and evil Events.'[1] A parallel development was La Bruyère's theory of taste: 'Il y a dans l'art un point de perfection, comme de bonté ou de maturité dans la nature. Celui qui le sent et qui l'aime a le goût parfait ; celui qui ne le sent pas, et qui aime en deça ou en delà, a le goût défectueux.'[2]

The practical objection to all cyclic theories was the difficulty of determining the precise moment when their ' point of perfection ' was attained. The difficulty was particularly acute in the linguistic field. ' Ev'ry Language', John Dennis pointed out, ' hath its particular period of Time to bring it to Perfection, I mean to all the Perfection of which that Language is capable. And they who are alive cannot possibly tell whether that period hath happen'd or not.'[3] It is not surprising therefore if differences of opinion occasionally manifest themselves as to the time when the English language reached the climax of its evolution. Swift put it in the reign of Charles I,[4] Henry Felton in that of

[1] Quoted in Clara Marburg's *Sir William Temple*, 1932.

[2] ' Des Ouvrages de l'Esprit ' (in *Les Caractères*).

[3] *Reflections upon a Lake Rhapsody*, 1711. Quotation from reprint in W. H. Durham, *Critical Essays, 1700-1725*, 1915.

[4] *A Proposal for Correcting, Improving and Ascertaining the English Tongue*, 1712.

Note [3]. *For Lake Rhapsody read Late Rhapsody*

Elizabeth,[1] and Godwin 'in the present reign' (i.e.
George III's).[2] But these writers were conscious
heretics. Orthodox opinion, from the Restoration
to the end of the eighteenth century, was agreed
with impressive unanimity that the flowering of the
English language was to be put at the end of the
seventeenth and the beginning of the eighteenth
centuries. This was Dryden's view,[3] and Gilbert
Burnet's,[4] Welsted's,[5] Tamworth Reresby's,[6] Oldmixon's,[7] Joseph Priestley's,[8] James Buchanan's,[9]
Goldsmith's,[10] Thomas Sheridan's,[11] Lord Mon-
boddo's,[12] and Noah Webster's.[13] And by a natural
analogy with Periclean Attic and Augustan Latin
this period became the English 'classical'[14] and
'Augustan'[15] age. The words were restricted in the

[1] I derive this from John Oldmixon's *An Essay on Criticism*, 1728,
p. 53. I have not found any such opinion in Felton's writings.

[2] *The Enquirer*, 1797, pp. 369–70. I am indebted for this and some
of the following references to S. A. Leonard's *The Doctrine of Correct-
ness in English Usage, 1700–1800*, 1929.

[3] 'The Dramatic Poetry of the Last Age' (added to part ii of *The
Conquest of Granada*, 1672).

[4] Quoted by Sir Thomas Pope Blount, *De Re Poetica*, 1694.

[5] Op. cit., p. xii.

[6] *A Miscellany of Ingenious Thoughts and Reflections*, 1721, p. 10.

[7] Op. cit., p. 55.    [8] *The Rudiments of English Grammar*, 1761.

[9] *A Regular English Syntax*, 1767.    [10] *The Bee*, 24 Nov. 1759.

[11] *General Dictionary of the English Language*, 1780.

[12] *Of the Origin and Progress of Language*, 1773–92.

[13] *A Letter on the Errors of English Grammar*, 1798.

[14] Welsted, op. cit., p. xiv ; Priestley, op. cit.

[15] The earliest instance the *N.E.D.* records is in 1819. But Anna
Seward's reference to the age of Pope, 'generally called the Augustan
Age' (*Gentleman's Magazine*, April 1789, p. 292), proves that it had
become current earlier. Its first occurrence seems to be in Goldsmith's
essay, 'An Account of the Augustan Age of England', *The Bee*,
24 Nov. 1759.

first instance to the language, and it was only later that they came to be applied to the literature. The Augustans themselves were very conscious that, though their language might have reached ' that Standard or Perfection, which dominates a Classical Age ',[1] they themselves had not. 'We are now so much refin'd, that how defective soever our Imaginations or Reasonings may be, yet our Language has fewer faults, and is more material and proper, than it was ever at any time before. The Materials to work with are good ; what we further require is Genius in the Workmen.'[2]

The ' point of perfection ' that the English language was considered to have reached between the years 1680 and 1730 was not altogether illusory. The language that Addison used for the periodical essay, that Pope used for *The Rape of the Lock* and Berkeley for *Hylas and Philonous*, that Swift used for *Gulliver's Travels* and Gay for *The Beggar's Opera*, was an instrument perfectly adapted for the purposes to which they put it. But it was not an instrument that they found ready-made for them. The English of Augustan poetry and prose was the culmination of a complicated process of discipline and refinement. Its secret is embodied in two words, 'polish ' and ' perspicuity '. 'Polish' was a condition of language. The reason that Welsted gives for his opinion that the English of his time was ' Standard or Perfection ' is that ' the most beautiful Polish is at length given to our Tongue '.[3] Welsted was

---

[1] Welsted, op. cit., p. viii.          [2] Ibid., p. xiv.
[3] Ibid., p. viii.

Line 5. *For* dominates *read* denominates

writing in 1724, but already by 1665 Cowley had projected an English Academy ' for the polishing of the English tongue '.[1] The project fell through, owing to the Plague and Cowley's death, but Thomas Sprat, his biographer, still considered ' some such aid' desirable in 1667. 'The Truth is', he remarks, in *The History of the Royal Society of London*, ' it [English] has been hitherto a little too carelessly handled, and, I think, has had less labour spent about its polishing than it deserves.'[2] 'Perspicuity', on the other hand, was a condition, *the* condition, of style and diction.

> To coin new words, or to restore the old,
> In southern bards is dangerous and bold ;
> But rarely, very rarely, will succeed,
> When minted on the other side of Tweed.
> Let perspicuity o'er all preside.[3]

'Perspicuity', Lord Kames agrees, 'ought not to be sacrificed to any other beauty whatever.'[4] 'Perspicuity', Blair repeats, 'is the fundamental quality of style.'[5]

The ideal that 'polish' and 'perspicuity' represent originated in a reaction from the looseness and vagueness of the language of the preceding period— with its 'words', as Hobbes complained, 'that

---

[1] See Evelyn's letter to Pepys reprinted in Spingarn, op. cit., vol. ii, p. 329.

[2] Selection reprinted in Spingarn, op. cit., vol. ii, p. 113.

[3] William Somerville, *Epistle to Mr. Thomson*, 1728.

[4] *Elements of Criticism. The Sixth Edition*, vol. ii, 1785, p. 19.

[5] *Lectures on Rhetoric and Belles Lettres*, vol. i, 1785. 'Perspicuity' certainly owed something of its prestige to Quintilian's *Nobis prima sit virtus perspicuitas*.

though of magnifique sound, yet (like the windy blisters of a troubled water) have no sense at all '.[1] The recommendations of the critics were therefore primarily negative. The obscurity in which Chapman had wished to be 'shadowed' became, to quote Tickell, 'of all qualities the most incongruous with the Nature of Poetry, since, unless Poetry is taken in at the first glance, it immediately loses its force and point '.[2] And the poetical ambiguities in which the metaphysicals had delighted were equally contraband. 'A vague or obscure expression', says Kames, 'is apt to gain favour with those who neglect to examine it with a critical eye. To some it carries the sense they relish the most ; and by suggesting various meanings at once, it is admired by others as concise and comprehensive.'[3] Rymer agreed that a 'doubtful meaning does not so well content the Reader as the certainty '.[4]

But there was a positive side to the movement, of which the most elaborate example is the third book of Locke's *Essay concerning Human Understanding*. A brief quotation from the chapter 'Of the Abuse of Words' will be sufficient to indicate Locke's general position :

The first and most palpable abuse is, the using of Words,

---

[1] *The Answer of Mr. Hobbes to Sir Will. D'Avenant's Preface Before Gondibert*, 1650. Reprinted Spingarn, op. cit., vol. ii, p. 63.

[2] *De Poesie Didactica*, an unpublished lecture delivered in 1711. English version in R. E. Tickell, *Thomas Tickell and the Eighteenth Century Poets*, 1931, p. 203.        [3] Op. cit., vol. ii, p. 21.

[4] 'The Preface of the Translator' (prefixed to the English version of R. Rapin's *Reflections on Aristotle's Treatise of Poesie*, 1674). Quotation from Spingarn's reprint, op. cit., vol. ii, p. 180.

Note [2]. *For De Poesie read De Poesi*

without clear and distinct Ideas. Another great abuse of Words is, Inconstancy in the use of them. It is hard to find a Discourse wherein one shall not observe, if he read with attention, the same Words used sometimes for one Collection of simple Ideas, and sometimes for another. Another abuse of Language is, an affected Obscurity, by either applying old Words, to new and unusual Significations; or introducing new and ambiguous Terms, without defining either; or else putting them so together, as may confound their ordinary meaning.

Locke, however, had been preceded by the Royal Society, who had ' exacted from all their members a close, natural way of speaking, positive expressions, a native easiness, bringing all things as near the Mathematical plainness as they can, and preferring the language of Artizans, Countrymen, and Merchants, before that of Wits or Scholars ',[1] and by Hobbes, who laid it down that ' in reasoning, a man must take heed of words; which beside the signification of what we imagine of their nature, have a signification also of the nature, disposition, and interest of the speaker; such as are the names of Vertues and Vices; For one man calleth *Wisdome*, what another calleth *feare*; and one *cruelty*, what another *justice*; one *prodigality*, what another *magnanimity*;

[1] Thomas Sprat, *The History of the Royal Society*, 1667. Quotation from Spingarn's reprint, op. cit., vol. ii, p. 118. The most ardent follower of the Royal Society's recommendations was a certain Nathaniel Fairfax, whose *Treatise of the Bulk and Selvedge of the World* (1674) excludes as far as possible all words borrowed from the learned or foreign languages. The ' Forespeech ' (Fairfax abhorred the learned word ' preface ') ' To the Reader' concludes with an enthusiastic plea for the adequacy of the ordinary spoken language as a medium for scientific communication.

and one *gravity*, what another *stupidity*, &c. And therefore such names can never be true grounds of any ratiocination.'[1]

The ultimate goal these reformers envisaged was a 'Mathematical plainness' of language. They hoped to scrape every word clean of its incrustation of connotation and 'polish' it to the purity of an algebraic symbol. Only then would the English language be fit to express with 'perspicuity' the clear and distinct ideas of the ruling Cartesian philosophy. Professor A. N. Whitehead once called the seventeenth century the mathematical century; the mathematization of language is certainly one of its most striking features. (It is characteristic of the period that John Wallis, the author of *Grammatica Linguae Anglicanae* (1653), should have been the Savilian Professor of Geometry at Oxford.)

The reformation of the language was an episode in a wider revolution. It was one aspect of a general attack upon the individualism and experimentalism of the first half of the seventeenth century. The right of every man to his own opinion, the heritage of the Reformation, had penetrated into the sphere of language. The watchword, in literature as in religion, had been 'inspiration'—'a dangerous word', said Davenant, 'which many have of late successfully us'd'.[2] It was precisely the kind of inspiration against which Davenant protested that had resulted in the confused babble of Charles I's

---

[1] *Leviathan*, 1651, ch. iv.
[2] 'The Author's Preface' (*Gondibert, An Heroick Poem*, 1650). Quotation from Spingarn's reprint, op. cit., vol. ii, p. 25.

reign and the Commonwealth. People had been so
busy and excited then expounding their own ideas
and emotions that they had not had time to inquire
whether they were intelligible or not. The impression that Milton's pamphlets, for example,
sometimes leave is of a crowd of people all talking
together, like the characters in Tchehov's plays.
And then, almost before they are aware of it, their
cherry orchard is cut down and they are swallowed
up, still talking, in the inferno of the Civil Wars!
The younger generation were determined to avoid
another such catastrophe—the difference between
the depositions of Charles I and James II is the
measure of their success. They had had more than
enough 'frequency of insignificant Speech'[1] and
'useless dispute and noise in the world'.[2] What
they set themselves to do therefore was to improve
the language as a medium of communication. Their
words were to be counters of an agreed value which
could pass from hand to hand and from one context
to another without changing their meaning. In
this way they believed that people would at last be
able to understand each other, to look into each
other's minds, and so to live and let live.[3] Their pro-
gramme was summed up by Hobbes: 'To conclude,
The Light of humane minds is Perspicuous Words,
but by exact definitions first snuffed and purged
from ambiguity; Reason is the pace; Encrease

[1] Hobbes, *Leviathan*, 1651, ch. i.
[2] Locke, *An Essay concerning Human Understanding*, Book ii, ch. ii.
[3] Samuel Parker (*A Discourse of Ecclesiastical Politie*, 1670) actually
advocated an Act of Parliament against 'fulsome and lushious Meta-
phors' as 'an effectual Cure of all our present Distempers'!

of Science, the way; and the Benefit of man-kind,
the end.'[1]   Ultimately therefore 'perspicuity' was
a duty to society.  It was not so much a doctrine
of style as a philosophy of conduct.  And as such
the contrast with the preceding period is apparent.
To the metaphysicals the claims of the individual
had been paramount; the standard was sincerity.
To the Augustans language was primarily a social
instrument and the test was intelligibility.  The difference is the key to the contradictions of tone and
method in their poetry.

Boileau used to say that Descartes had cut poetry's
throat,[2] and the linguistic ideals of Descartes's English contemporaries and followers were certainly
apparently inimical to poetry.  'The Elizabethans
created a style in poetry, and by misapplying some
of its qualities formed their prose.  The Annians
created a style in prose, and wrenched its characteristics to form their poetry.'[3]  'Dryden and Pope are
classics not of our poetry but of our prose.'[4]  But
to rebut such charges as these it is only necessary
to correlate the Augustans' ideal of 'perspicuity'
with another key-word of theirs—'energy'.

> But who did ever in French Authors see
> The comprehensive English Energy?
> The weighty Bullion of One Sterling Line,
> Drawn to French Wire, would thro' whole Pages shine.

[1] *Leviathan*, 1651, ch. v.
[2] See J. B. Rousseau's letter to Brosette, 14 July 1711.
[3] Rossetti, *Collected Works*, vol. i, 1901, p. 511.
[4] Matthew Arnold, 'The Study of Poetry' (in *Essays in Criticism. Second Series*).

I speak my private but impartial sense,
With Freedom, and (I hope) without offence;
For I'le Recant, when France can shew me Wit,
As strong as Ours, and as succinctly Writ.[1]

*Energy, weight, strength, succinctness* (or 'condensation')[2]—these are the central qualities of Augustan poetry. 'Wit, Ingenuity, and Learning in Verse, even Elegancy it self, though that comes neerest, are one thing, true Native Poetry is another; nay, though all the Laws of Heroic Poem, all the Laws of Tragedy were exactly observed, yet still this *tout entrajeant*, this Poetic Energie, if I may so call it, would be required to give life to all the rest.'[3]

A few examples may be helpful at this point. I choose Dryden's 'Secular Masque':

> Thy Sword within the Scabbard keep,
> And let Mankind agree;
> Better the World were fast asleep,
> Than kept awake by Thee.

And Pope's 'Elegy':

> Is it, in heav'n, a crime to love too well?
> To bear too tender, or too firm a heart,
> To act a Lover's or a Roman's part?
> Is there no bright reversion in the sky,
> For those who greatly think, or bravely die?

[1] Roscommon, *An Essay on Translated Verse*, 1684. Quotation from reprint in Spingarn, op. cit., vol. ii, p. 298.

[2] 'Mr. Pope's chief excellence lies in what I would term consolidating or condensing sentences, yet preserving ease and perspicuity' (Shenstone, *Works*, vol. ii, 1764, p. 14).

[3] Edward Phillips, 'Preface' (to *Theatrum Poetarum*, 1675). Quotation from reprint in Spingarn, op. cit., vol. ii, p. 271.

And Johnson's 'Vanity of Human Wishes':

> His fall was destin'd to a barren strand,
> A petty fortress, and a dubious hand;
> He left the name, at which the world grew pale,
> To point a moral, or adorn a tale.

The quality of style that unites these three passages is clearly 'energy'. They impose themselves, one and all, with something of the irresistible force of a battering-ram. What is not so clear is that the 'energy' of the poetry is closely dependent upon the "perspicuity" of the diction. The Augustan achievement was by shearing words of their secondary and irrelevant associations to release the full emphasis of their primary meanings. The connotations, instead of blurring the denotations, reinforced them. The poetry of Dryden and Pope differs therefore from earlier and later English poetry in that it is not a poetry of suggestion but of statement. The 'meaning' of a metaphysical or a romantic poem, the totality of impressions created by it, is *implicit*—an obscure complex in which the contributions of logic, rhythm, and emotional suggestion are almost inextricable. But an Augustan poem is *explicit*. The meaning is, and must be, on the surface, and in so far as the wording or rhythm introduces subsidiary elements, which distract the attention from the structure of the poem, it ceases to be purely Augustan. (Pope's 'bright reversion' may perhaps be accused of this.) The bareness of diction, the absence of metaphor, and the metrical monotony of Augustan poetry were therefore deliberate and necessary. They ensure the precision and the economy of its strokes.

## IV

I have been principally concerned in the preceding sections with the diction of the Elizabethan, metaphysical, and Augustan poets. But diction is only one element, if the most important, in a poetic style. A poem is not an accumulation of words but an accumulation of words in a certain order. It is to the *structure* therefore of sixteenth- and seventeenth-century poetry that I propose now to turn. How did these poets arrange their words? Is it possible to trace a process of evolution in poetic structure parallel to the evolution of diction that we have already considered?

The problem will be most conveniently approached *a posteriori*. Here is an early Elizabethan poem— it is, of course, Wyatt's 'The lover sheweth how he is forsaken of such as he somtime enjoyed'. Can we analyse its mode of progression? Can we define the way in which it hangs together?

> They flee from me, that somtime did me seke
>    With naked fote stalkyng within my chamber.
> Once have I seen them gentle, tame, and meke,
> That now are wild, and do not once remember
> That sometyme they have put them selves in danger,
> To take bread at my hand, and now they range,
> Busily sekyng in continuall change.
>    Thanked be fortune, it hath bene otherwise
> Twenty tymes better : but once especiall,
> In thinne aray, after a pleasant gyse,

Line 16. *For* an early Elizabethan poem *read* a Tottel's Miscellany poem

When her loose gowne did from her shoulders fall,
And she me caught in her armes long and small,
And therwithall, so swetely did me kysse,
And softly sayd : deare hart, how like you this?
    It was no dreame : for I lay broade awakyng.
But all is turnde now through my gentlenesse
Into a bitter fashion of forsakyng :
And I have leave to go of her goodnesse,
And she also to use newfanglenesse.
But, sins that I unkyndly so am served :
How like you this, what hath she now deserved?

The theme of Wyatt's poem, its 'argument', is
simple. 'The poet laments the inconstancy of his
mistress and contrasts her cruelty now with her
former kindnesses.' And the theme is developed by
a series of variations that are almost equivalent to
repetitions. Lines 1, 2 state the theme in general
terms ; lines 3–7 develop the antithesis (the mistress
who was once *tame* is now *wild*) ; lines 8–15 exem-
plify one half of the antithesis (the mistress was
once kind), and lines 16–19 the other half (she is now
cruel) ; and the concluding couplet sums the situation up. The structural scheme of the poem is
therefore an initial statement of the theme followed
by a symmetrical development of its implications.[1]

By the side of Wyatt's poem I shall put Thomas
Carew's ' Song. To my inconstant Mistris ', a poem
on a similar subject but written a hundred years
later and in the metaphysical style :

---

[1] Professor de Selincourt (*Oxford Spenser*, 1912, p. lxvi) has defined
the 'sustaining principle' of Spenser's verse as ' a slow circling movement that continually returned upon itself '.

When thou, poore excommunicate
    From all the joyes of love, shalt see
The full reward, and glorious fate,
    Which my strong faith shall purchase me,
    Then curse thine own inconstancy.
A fayrer hand then thine, shall cure
    That heart, which thy false oathes did wound ;
And to my soule, a soule more pure
    Than thine, shall by Loves hand be bound,
    And both with equall glory crown'd.
Then shalt thou weepe, entreat, complaine
    To Love, as I did once to thee ;
When all thy teares shall be as vaine
    As mine were then, for thou shalt bee
    Damn'd for thy false Apostasie.

It will at once be seen that Carew's theme is more complicated than Wyatt's, since it involves the future with the present and the past. ' The poet has been abandoned by his mistress, but he foresees a reversal of their roles when it will be his turn to be triumphant and cruel and hers to be rejected and miserable.' But the essential difference between Wyatt's poem and Carew's, from the point of view of structure, is not in the themes but in their development of them. Wyatt's theme is stated in his first line and the rest of the poem only expands and elucidates its implications. Carew's theme, on the other hand, is coextensive with his poem. We do not know what the subject of his poem is until we have completed it. The first verse presents a constant lover prophesying to his inconstant mistress a glorious future for himself from which she is to be excluded. But the nature of the lover's glory-to-be

is not defined until the second verse, and the reversal of their roles, which gives point to the
mistress's exclusion from it, is retained until the
third verse. We may call this mode of structure
organic. The poem *grows* as it progresses; the
theme develops from verse to verse and is not complete until the poem has ended.

An Augustan version of Wyatt's and Carew's
poems is provided by Congreve's 'Song':

> False though she be to me and Love,
>  I'll ne'er pursue Revenge;
> For still the Charmer I approve,
>  Tho' I deplore her Change.
>
> In Hours of Bliss we oft have met,
>  They could not always last;
> And though the present I regret,
>  I'm grateful for the past.

Like Carew, but unlike Wyatt, Congreve includes
the future in his poem with the present and the
past. He waives the future, he regrets the present,
he is grateful for the past. And like Wyatt, but unlike Carew, he announces his theme in the first two
lines. But there the likenesses end, and Congreve's
poem is developed in quite a different manner from
that of either of the earlier poets. Its structure is
not repetitive or organic but logical. The poem
consists of a conclusion—'I forgive my inconstant
mistress'—followed by the three premises from
which that conclusion has been deduced—'I still
love her', 'we have been happy together', and
'changes are inevitable'. The last six lines are
really the *justification* of his first two lines.

Our analyses have left us with three types of poetic structure: the repetitive (Wyatt's), the organic (Carew's), and the logical (Congreve's). And these three types can be shown, I believe, to be the representative modes of the Elizabethan, metaphysical, and Augustan styles.[1] For the moment, however, it will be sufficient to note the parallelism of diction and structure in the three periods.

The diction of the Elizabethan poets was characterized, as we have seen, by the glosses and amplifications of 'copie'. Their words and phrases are reinforced by secondary words and phrases which seem to add little or nothing to the original meaning:

Beside his head there satt a faire young man,
(This announces the theme, as in music.)
Of wondrous beauty and of freshest yeares,
(The fair young man was fair and young.)
Whose tender bud to blossom new began,
(The fair young man was young.)
And florish faire above his equal peers.
(The fair young man was fair, fairer even than his equals, who were also his peers.)[2]

In Spenser, therefore, as in the preceding passage, and the other Elizabethan poets the repetitive structure is inextricable from the repetitive diction.

---

[1] An analysis of a considerable number of sixteenth- and seventeenth-century poems has shown that, in addition to the three main types (illustrated above), there are some hybrid or transitional types. Campion's 'Follow thy fair sun, unhappy shadow', for example, exhibits a form of structure that is a sort of compromise between the repetitive and the organic modes.

[2] Sir Walter Raleigh, *Milton*, 1915, pp. 200-1.

The formula in either case is a series of variations upon a single initial idea. The only difference is a difference of scale. Elizabethan diction and Elizabethan structure are two aspects of the same process, the one functioning within the smaller unit of the sentence and the other within the larger unit of the poem. And a similar relationship can be demonstrated between the vividness of the metaphysical style, its 'life', and the organic mode of structure, and the 'perspicuity' and logical structure of the Augustans.

# POETIC DICTION AND THE SUBLIME

## I

THE motto that Collins has prefixed to his *Odes* (1747) is Pindar's εἴην εὑρησιεπής. 'May I be devizer of poetic diction!' And the ambition was not by any means confined to Collins. The whole poetic output of the eighteenth century, with the exception of the light verse and a few freaks like Blake and Burns, is swaddled in the, for us, wet blanket of 'poetic diction'. It is not too much to say, indeed, that it constitutes the one almost insuperable bar to an appreciation of eighteenth-century poetry to-day. We can enjoy the matter and we can endure the metre—the diction defeats us. And yet 'poetic diction' is of the essence of eighteenth-century poetry. It was 'poetic diction', as much as anything, that made Thomson, Young, Gray, Collins, and Smart what they are, and unless we can appreciate its function we cannot begin to understand their poems. At present these poets are read, if at all, in spite of their diction. But the absurdity of such a proceeding should be obvious. It is as though I was reading a foreign language and would not look up in a dictionary the words I did not understand!

The first point to be made in an apology for the eighteenth century is that there were *two* poetic dictions. It is because the two theories are still confused that the several strands in eighteenth-century

Line 3. *For* devizer *read* a devizer

poetry have never been properly disentangled and the period is dismissed in despair as a chaos of muddled and divided intentions. The earlier theory was merely negative : there are some words which are *not* suitable for poetry. '(To begin with words) the first Indiscretion is, The use of such words as to the Readers of Poesie (which are commonly Persons of the best Quality) are not sufficiently known. Forein words, till by long use they become vulgar, are unintelligible to them. Also the names of Instruments and Tools of Artificers, and words of Art.'² There is no difficulty here. The test was intelligibility, and neologisms and technical and scientific terms were objectionable because they were unfamiliar. A later development of the theory was that some words were *too* familiar. The notorious example is Johnson's comment on the lines in *Macbeth* :

> Come, thick night,
> And pall thee in the dunnest smoke of hell,
> That my keen knife see not the wound it makes.

*Dunnest*, Johnson objected, was 'an epithet now seldom heard but in the stable', and *knife* was 'an instrument used by butchers and cooks in the meanest employments'.² And Johnson had been preceded by Dryden. 'If I should translate it [*mollis amaracus*] *sweet marjoram*, as the word signifies', Dryden writes, in the dedication of *The Aeneis*, 'the reader would

---

¹ Hobbes, 'To the Reader concerning The Vertues of an Heroique Poem' (prefixed to *Homer's Odysses*, 1675). Quotation from reprint in Spingarn, op. cit., vol. ii, p. 68.
² *The Rambler*, 26 Oct. 1751.

Line 12. *For* Art'.² *read* Art'.¹

think I had mistaken Virgil: for those village words, as I may call them, give us a mean idea of the thing.'

It is easy, of course, to make Johnson and Dryden look ridiculous ; they had no business to rewrite Shakespeare and Virgil. But the theory they mis-applied is comprehensible. 'The question is,.how far a Poet, in pursuing the description or image of an action, can attach himself to little circumstances, without vulgarity or trifling ? what particulars are proper, and enliven the image; or what are imper-tinent and clog it?'[1] The negative theory of poetic diction was a consistent attempt to differentiate words by their associations. 'Many words there are in every tongue, which are not used, except by illiterate persons, or on very familiar occasions, or in order to express what the decorum of polite society requires that we conceal.' These 'mean' words were contraband in poetry. But 'those words are not mean, which are so necessary at all times, that it is impossible to speak without them on any sub-ject. And most of the classical words in every tongue are of this character. Words are not mean, because they are plain.'[2]

The theory was a natural extension of the Augustan position. The Augustan poets, as we have seen, wished to use the associations of words as a reinforcement of their primary meanings. They tended therefore to avoid familiar words because of the unmanageable range of their associations and

---

[1] Pope, 'Postscript' (to *The Odyssey of Homer*, vol. v, 1726, p. 272).
[2] James Beattie, *Dissertations Moral and Critical*, 1783, pp. 648–9.

unfamiliar words for the opposite reason that they had next to no associations at all. 'Words too familiar, or too remote, defeat the purpose of a poet. From those sounds which we hear on small or on coarse occasions, we do not easily receive strong impressions or delightful images; and words to which we are nearly strangers, whenever they occur, draw that attention on themselves which they should transmit to things.'[1]

The term 'poetic diction' should be restricted to the positive theory: there are some words which are *only* (or *especially*) suitable for poetry. But this was a later development. The Augustan critics did not distinguish, theoretically at any rate, between the dictions of poetry and prose. They assumed, and the practice of their contemporaries generally bears them out, that there can only be one literary language, though there may be several applications of it. The positive theory of poetic diction, as we find it, for example, in Gray, was a direct contradiction of this assumption. 'As to matter of style,' Gray writes to West, 'I have this to say: the language of the age is never the language of poetry; except among the French. Our poetry, on the contrary, has a language peculiar to itself.'[2] The thesis therefore of the positive theory was that there are, or should be, two distinct literary languages (each with various subdivisions), the language of poetry and the language of prose. It was not

---

[1] Johnson, 'Dryden' (*Lives of the Poets*, 1781).
[2] The letter, written in 1742, is reprinted in E. D. Jones, *English Critical Essays*, 1922, p. 310.

denied that the two languages, or dialects, must overlap, but the emphasis, in this theory, was upon their differences. The greater the difference, the better—that is, the more poetical—the poetry.

The ambition of the neo-classic critics, from the time of the Renaissance, had been to confine literature within certain prescribed forms. Tragedy was tragedy, comedy was comedy, and never the twain should meet. 'Drama must be either tragic or comic, it must obey the very definite rules set down for each kind, and no other form of dramatic expression is possible or allowable.'[1] But this process of specialization had originally been restricted to problems of matter and form. It was not until the eighteenth century that it began to include the province of expression. It was only then that the centre of theoretical interest shifted from the common denominator in language, that central core of words which is shared by every department of literature and thought, to the specialized form. The vocabulary of poetic diction can be paralleled in the numerous technical terms of science, philosophy, and politics that were coined in the eighteenth century. The motives that led the chemists to create a word like 'phlogiston' (first used in 1733) were ultimately identical with those that induced Thomson and the rest to call fishes a 'finny tribe'. Both words could have been replaced by others already in use, but they were not mere synonyms. By restricting a general notion to a particular field they represented a gain in precision. 'Phlogiston' did

[1] H. S. Davies, *Realism in the Drama*, 1934, p. 31.

not just mean the principle of inflammability, but that principle as used in the science of chemistry; and the 'finny tribe' was fishes considered solely as the subject of poetry. The tendency was therefore a natural development of the doctrine of 'perspicuity'. That doctrine, as originally formulated, had been that there could be no possibility of obscurity or ambiguity if every word were restricted to a single universally accepted meaning. But the condition proved unrealizable. A word cannot be isolated from the contexts in which it is used, and if its contexts vary its shades of meaning will vary with them. The specialization of vocabularies, of which the development of a specifically poetic diction was a part, was an attempt to overcome this difficulty. For obviously, if every word could be limited to a particular context no variations in its meaning could arise.[1]

The critical difference therefore between the negative and positive theories of poetic diction is that the former was relative (a word's suitability or unsuitability depended upon the subject) and the latter absolute (some words were *always* suitable). 'There are certain words in every language particularly adapted to the poetical expression; some from the image or idea they convey to the imagination, and some from the effect they have upon the ear.'[2]

[1] Joan Platt, 'The Development of English Colloquial Idiom during the Eighteenth Century' (*Review of English Studies*, Jan., April 1926), includes an interesting discussion of the 'tendency to specialize the meanings of words, in order to use them in restricted senses arising as the needs of expression multiply, in the eighteenth century'.

[2] Goldsmith, 'Poetry distinguished from other Writing' (in *Essays*).

That was the pure doctrine of poetic diction. There was a magical cohort of words that could be *guaranteed* to produce a poetical effect. 'We acknowledge him [Homer] the Father of Poetical Diction,' Pope wrote, using the term, I believe, for the second time in English,[1] 'the first who taught that Language of the Gods to Men.'[2] Poetic diction, that is to say, was divine in itself. It immortalized the poems into which it could be inserted.

The theory was not often pushed to these extremes, but it is true to say that this diction, in contrast with the diction of the Augustans, always has something subsidiary and external about it. 'There is this material difference', Robert Lloyd pointed out (in 1756), 'between the former and present age of poetry; that the writers in the first thought poetically; in the last, they only express themselves so. Modern poets seem to me more to study the manner how they shall write, than what is to be written.'[3] 'The most obvious Defect in our Poetry,' Aaron Hill agreed, 'and I think the greatest it is liable to, is, that we study Form, and neglect Matter.'[4]

---

[1] Its first occurrence seems to be in John Dennis's *The Advancement and Reformation of Modern Poetry*, 1701, ch. v.

[2] 'Preface' (to *The Iliad*, vol. i, 1715). Pope considered the adjective the most important element in poetic diction. 'To throw his Language more out of Prose, Homer seems to have affected the Compound-Epithets' (ibid.). 'Epithets are of vast service to this effect, and the right use of these is often the only expedient to render the narrative poetical' (*Odyssey*, 'Postscript', 1726).

[3] *The Connoisseur*, 17 June 1756.

[4] 'Preface to Mr. Pope' (prefixed to *The Creation*, 1720, p. vi). This divorce between matter and manner was bolstered up by an analogy with the art of painting. *Ut pictura poesis*:

Note [1]. For *The Advancement* . . . 1701, ch. v *read Remarks on a Book Entituled, Prince Arthur*, 1696, Preface

The diction of the Augustans was inherent and structural; poetic diction is primarily ornamental, an afterthought. Reading some of the eighteenth-century poets one has the curious feeling that there is a gap, an almost measurable time-interval, between the thought and the words. The words do not seem to be the expression of the thought so much as its translation into another medium.[1]

But before we condemn poetic diction outright

> Poets are limners of another kind,
> To copy out Idaeas in the Mind;
> Words are the paint by which their Thoughts are shown.

(George Granville, *An Essay upon Unnatural Flights in Poetry*, 1701; reprinted Spingarn, op. cit., vol. iii, p. 292.) And the transition was simple from words being paint to words being colour—that 'Beauty of Colouring, in which consists chiefly the Poets Art' (Edward Bysshe, 'Preface' to *The Art of English Poetry*, 1702). But the transition once made and 'colouring' (i.e. diction) once isolated, it was natural to separate it from, and even oppose it to, design. As a painter added colours to his sketch, so a poet superinduced poetic diction upon his 'thoughts'. 'Expression', Dryden pronounced (*Essays*, ed. W. P. Ker, vol. ii, p. 147), 'and all that belongs to words, is that in a poem which colouring is in a picture. Our author calls Colouring, *lena sororis*: in plain English, the bawd of her sister, the design or drawing: she clothes, she dresses her up, she paints her.'

[1] The earliest elaborate attack upon poetic diction is in John Weston's 'An Essay on the Superiority of Dryden's Versification over that of Pope and of the Moderns' (prefixed to Weston's translation, 1788, of John Morfitt's *Philotoxi Ardenae*). The crucial passage is: 'But, as He [Pope] was supposed to have improved upon his Master, our Poets seem ambitious of improving on theirs.—He rejected every Thing that was not rich; They reject every Thing that is not brilliant.—He is every where clear and manly; They not unfrequently torture into Obscurity, and refine into Imbecility. To confirm and illustrate my Observations, by selecting Instances of harsh Construction and fantastic Inversion—Tinsel Phrases and tinkling Compound-Epithets—were a Task as easy as it were unpleasant. . . . Suffice it, therefore, to observe, that the modern System appears decisively to exclude every Mode of Expression from Poetry which is so unlucky as to find a Place in Prose.'

we must inquire what the function was that it was intended to perform. Judged by the standards of its own time, instead of by those of the nineteenth century, it may be rational and defensible. It is possible that the blunted and ornamental diction was deliberate, and that a more pointed and natural diction might have interfered with other and more fundamental intentions. For it must not be forgotten that the specifically poetic diction of poets like Thomson and Young is only a part of the diction that is used in their poems. It is an element in the total impression that this poetry conveys; it is not the whole poetry.

The problem is of peculiar perplexity because the two theories of poetic diction, though logically one is derived from the·other, overlap chronologically. The negative, or Augustan, theory survived in Johnson and Lloyd, and even in Cowper. The positive theory had been adumbrated by Addison.[1] And Pope wavered between the two. Nevertheless, a broad distinction is observable. There are two main groups or·schools of poetry to one or other of which the major poets of the century can all be affiliated. 'I think it is not difficult to perceive', Vicesimus Knox writes in 1782, 'that the admirers of English poetry are divided into two parties. On one side are the lovers and imitators of Spenser and Milton; and on the other, those of Dryden, Boileau, and Pope.'[2]

[1] *The Spectator*, No. 285, contains such suggestions as ' a poet should take particular care to guard himself against idiomatic ways of speaking'.

[2] *Essays, Moral and Literary*, No. 129. A similar division was made by Thomas Warton (in his ' Preface ', p. x, to Milton's *Minor Poems*, 1785): ' A visible revolution succeeded in the general cast and character

As examples of the first group Knox mentions Gray, the Wartons, and Mason, and of the second Johnson, Goldsmith, Anstey, and Hayley.

Knox's second group—the party of Dryden, Boileau, and Pope—offers no difficulty. They are the Augustans, the advocates of a negative theory of poetic diction. His first group (to which we may add Young, Thomson, Collins, and Smart) is less amenable to definition. Gray and Collins, and even Thomson and Young, have been called 'preromantics', 'heralds of the romantic revival'. But the label, though plausible, is, I maintain, misleading. It is true that some 'romantic' lines can be found in these poets :

> Prisoner of earth, and pent beneath the moon. (*Young.*)
> Narcissus fair,
> As o'er the fabled fountain hanging still.   (*Thomson.*)
> While I lie welt'ring on the ozier'd shore.   (*Collins.*)

But lines such as these, which are in any case exceptional, are not romantic except when excerpted from their setting. Replace them in the original contexts and the romantic glow leaves them. They are essentially artificial and 'literary', 'cut and slightly withered flowers stuck into sand'.[1]

of the national composition. Our versification contracted a new colouring, a new structure and phraseology ; and the school of Milton rose in emulation of the school of Pope.'

[1] Collins's line is of course a reminiscence of 'Lycidas'. The poems of Mason and the Wartons, and to a less degree Gray and Collins, are almost a mosaic of borrowed phrases. Lloyd (*The Connoisseur*, 8 May 1755), an Augustan in his sympathies, complained that 'their whole business is imitation'. But Hurd, who may be considered the critical spokesman of the 'pre-romantic' group, had anticipated the criticism in the important *Discourse of Poetical Imitation* (1753).

Romantic poetry invites an analogy with music. But the art with which the poetry of the 'pre-romantics' is comparable is rather architecture. The only equivalent I can find to the impression of orderly disorder and artificial excitement which the poetry of Thomson, Young, Gray, and Collins, in its most characteristic moments, makes on me is that produced by baroque architecture:

> The disenchanted earth
> Lost all her lustre.   Where her glittering towers?
> Her golden mountains, where? all darken'd down
> To naked waste; a dreary vale of tears;
> The great magician's dead !   (*Young*.)

> Or, in some hollow'd Seat,
> 'Gainst which the big Waves beat,
> Hear drowning Sea-men's Cries in Tempests brought !
> (*Collins*.)

> Cold is Cadwallo's tongue,
> That hush'd the stormy main ;
> Brave Urien sleeps upon his craggy bed :
> Mountains, ye mourn in vain
> Modred, whose magic song
> Made huge Plinlimmon bow his cloud-top'd head.
> (*Gray*.)

This poetry, in comparison with that of the Augustans, is hectic and restless, but its restlessness is as deliberate and calculated as the Augustan serenity. The structural outline, the composition, is firm and clear, though the emotions released, instead of being centripetal as in classical poetry, are centrifugal. It is a poetry, in other words, not of concentration but of expansion. But the expansion is orderly and, though it hints at things outside the range of reference in which it is bound, its hints are not pursued to the point where they would endanger the central unity. A combination of movement with repose is also the key-note of baroque architecture:

To give the picturesque its grandest scope, and yet to subdue it to architectural law—this was the baroque experiment and it is achieved. The baroque is not afraid to startle and arrest. Like Nature, it is fantastic, unexpected, varied and grotesque. It is all this in the highest degree. But, unlike Nature, it remains subject rigidly to the laws of scale and composition. It enlarged their scope, but would not modify their stringency. It is not, therefore, in any true sense accidental, irregular, or wild. It makes—for the parallel is exact—a more various use of discords and suspensions, and it stands in a closely similar relation to the simpler and more static style which preceded it, as the later music to the earlier. It enlarged the classic formula by developing within it the principle of movement. But the movement is logical. For baroque architecture is always logical: it is logical as an aesthetic construction even where it most neglects the logic of material construction. It insisted on coherent purpose, and its greatest extravagances of design were neither unconsidered nor inconsistent. *It intellectualised the picturesque.*[1]

And the parallel with baroque architecture throws a new light upon the problem of poetic diction. For the function of the invocations, the personifications, and the stock phrases of Thomson, Young, and the others is, I believe, identical with that of baroque ornament. The arguments that have been used to defend the one may also be utilized for the other:

[1] Geoffrey Scott, *The Architecture of Humanism*, 1914, p. 86.

The detail of the baroque style is rough. It is not finished with the loving care of the *quattrocento*, or even of the somewhat clumsy Gothic. It often makes no effort to represent anything in particular, or even to commit itself to any definite form. It makes shift with tumbled draperies which have no serious relation to the human structure; it delights in vague volutes that have no serious relation to the architectural structure. It is rapid and inexact. But the purpose was exact, though it required 'inexact' architecture for its fulfilment. They [the baroque architects] wished to communicate, through architecture, a sense of exultant vigour and overflowing strength . . . the parts should appear to flow together, merge into one another, spring from one another, and form, as it were, a fused gigantic organism through which currents of continuous vigour might be conceived to run. A lack of individual distinctness in the parts—a lack of the intellectual differentiation which Bramante, for example, might have given them—was thus not a negative neglect, but a positive demand. Their 'inexactness' was a necessary invention.[1]

The baroque style is rapid and inexact: it is rapid *because* it is inexact. And so with poetic diction. The style of such poets as Thomson, Young, Gray, and Collins is a rapid style; but their diction is conventional. And the diction is conventional *because* the style is rapid. A more precise and concrete diction would have destroyed the impression of rapidity that the style conveys. It is only because the individual words attract so little attention to themselves that the poetry is able to attain its unrivalled and almost headlong sense of movement.

[1] Ibid., pp. 147–8.

## II

The complex of qualities that I have defined as baroque was distinguished at the time as the Sublime. But the word was used in a more limited sense than it bears now, or than Longinus had assigned to it. Longinus, Beattie noted in his interesting 'Illustrations on Sublimity', 'has used the word Hupsos in a more general sense, than is commonly annexed to the term Sublimity; not always distinguishing what is sublime from what is elegant or beautiful'.[1] To the baroque critics, on the other hand, the two qualities of beauty and sublimity were opposed and mutually exclusive. Beauty, according to one critic, afforded a 'refined Delight', whereas sublimity created an 'exalted Disposition'.[2] Beauty was an artificial product, sublimity a natural phenomenon. 'The Sublime in Writing is no more than a Description of the Sublime in Nature, and as it were painting to the Imagination what Nature herself offers to the Senses.'[3] The Sublime was characterized therefore by 'Vastness' and 'Magnitude', though it failed of its effect if it did not also possess 'Uniformity'.[4]

In *A Philosophical Inquiry into the Origin of our Ideas of the Sublime and the Beautiful* (1757) Burke attempted to derive these sensations from the emotions of love (the social instincts) and fear (the self-regarding instincts) respectively:

[1] *Dissertations*, 1783, p. 605.
[2] John Baillie, *An Essay on the Sublime*, 1747, p. 36.
[3] Ibid., pp. 3, 6.                    [4] Ibid., p. 9.

The passions which belong to self-preservation turn on pain and danger; they are simply painful when their causes immediately affect us; they are delightful when we have an idea of pain and danger, without being actually in such circumstances. Whatever excites this delight, I call *sublime*. The second head to which the passions are referred with relation to their final cause is society. The passion subservient to this is called love, and its object is beauty; which is a name I shall apply to all such qualities in things as induce in us a sense of affection and tenderness, or some other passion the most nearly resembling these.[1]

Burke's argument, however, though of epoch-making importance in the history of aesthetics, is less interesting as a clue to the characteristics of baroque poetry than the consequences he drew from it. The most important of these riders was the identification of sublimity with obscurity. A demonstration that 'terror is in all cases whatsoever, either more openly or latently, the ruling principle of the sublime'[2] is followed by the conclusion that 'To make anything very terrible, obscurity seems in general to be necessary'.[3] 'In reality, a great clearness helps but little towards affecting the passions, as it is in some sort an enemy to all enthusiasms',[4] and 'A clear idea is another name for a little idea'.[5] Beauty, on the other hand, sublimity's opposite, of which littleness was one of the essential qualities,[6] 'should not be obscure'.[7]

The depreciations of beauty and clarity were

[1] Part I, section xviii.
[2] Part II, section ii.
[3] Part II, section iii.
[4] Part II, section iv.
[5] Part II, section iv.
[6] Part III, section xiii.
[7] Part III, section xxvii.

equivalent, in the sphere of language, to a denial of the Augustan ideal of intelligibility.[1] The baroque standard was 'strength', or 'force', rather than 'perspicuity' and 'polish'. 'It may be observed', Burke noted, 'that very polished languages, and such as are praised for their superior clearness and perspicuity, are generally deficient in strength. The French language has that perfection and that defect. Whereas the oriental tongues, and in general the languages of most unpolished people, have a great force and energy of expression.'[2] And Knox agreed that 'the amplification of a sentence, though it may add to its perspicuity, frequently diminishes its force'.[3] It had come to be realized that 'perspicuity' and 'force', the kind of force that is discoverable in folk-poetry and the primitive epics, were incompatible qualities which defeated each other's purposes, and with the realization there had developed a tolerance, and then an appreciation, of obscurity in poetry. Knox, indeed, considered the obscurity of the Authorized Version ('the sublimest and most interesting books in the English language') its principal 'poetical merit'.[4] But the obscurity of

---

[1] Joseph Warton used the Sublime simply as a stick to beat Pope with : 'The Sublime and the Pathetic are the two chief nerves of all genuine poesy. What is there transcendently Sublime or Pathetic in Pope ?' (*An Essay on the Genius and Writings of Pope*, 2 vols., 1782; 'Dedication'.) Pope's one wholly baroque poem, 'Eloisa to Abelard'—which Pope himself described, in a letter to Dr. Cowper, as having 'more of that Descriptive, & (if I may so say) Enthusiastic Spirit, wch is the Character of ye Ancient Poets'—is partially excepted by Warton, who allows that the high mass is 'sublime' (vol. i, p. 336).

[2] Op. cit., Part V, section vii.

[3] Op. cit., No. 44.                    [4] Ibid., No. 167.

the baroque poets themselves was a new kind of obscurity and very different from the earlier obscurity of the metaphysical poets. The metaphysical style had been obscure because of its 'ambiguity', its richness of content, its superimposed layers of meaning. Poetical ambiguity, however, was condemned by the baroque critics as whole-heartedly as by the Augustans. Beattie, for example, while granting that 'where sublimity with horror is intended, a certain degree of darkness may have a good effect', criticizes a passage in Young's *Night Thoughts* because 'it is rather ambiguous than obscure'.[1] Baroque poetry was obscure because it was abrupt and incoherent—or because it seemed so in comparison with the lucidity and order of the Augustans.[2]

Thomson's 'Hymn' (appended to *The Seasons*), the sublimity of which is guaranteed by Beattie, 'if we overlook an unguarded word or two',[3] may be taken as typical of the baroque method:

From World to World, the vital Ocean round,
On Nature write with every Beam His Praise.
The Thunder rolls: be hush'd the prostrate World;
While Cloud to Cloud returns the solemn Hymn.
Bleat out afresh, ye Hills; ye mossy Rocks,

[1] Op. cit., p. 638.
[2] The qualification is necessary. The modern reader does not find Gray's 'The Progress of Poesy' and 'The Bard' especially difficult; but for Johnson they were 'two compositions at which the readers of poetry were at first content to gaze in mute amazement. Some that tried them confessed their inability to understand them' ('Gray' in *Lives of the Poets*).
[3] Op. cit., p. 626.

Retain the Sound : the broad responsive Low,
Ye Valleys, raise; for the GREAT SHEPHERD reigns;
And his unsuffering Kingdom yet will come.

Read slowly and in an excerpt the tawdriness of
Thomson's lines becomes evident. But they should
not be read slowly. Surrender yourself to the
vehemence of the verse and the confused grandeur
of the images, and a peculiar condition of nervous
excitement, the baroque thrill, will supervene. That
is 'sublimity'. The technical basis of that thrill has
been acutely, if unintentionally, exposed by Burke.
'The mind is hurried out of itself by a crowd of
great and confused images, which affect because
they are crowded and confused. For separate them,
and you lose much of the greatness; and join them,
and you infallibly lose the clearness.'[1] The poem's
'greatness', that is, is dependent first of all on its
'hurry' and secondly on its 'confusion'. And these
qualities are ultimately traceable to an absence of
structure and cohesion. Thomson's 'Hymn' is
virtually a roll-call, in which the poet summons the
forces of nature—the winds, the sea, the flowers,
the forests, the corn, the stars, and the rest—to unite
in praising God. But is there any reason why the
roll-call should be in this particular order? Would
not any other order, provided it were equally for-
tuitous, really be just as effective? The disorderli-
ness, however, here, and in Smart's *Song to David*,
and indeed in all baroque poetry, is actually the

[1] Op. cit., Part II, section [iv]. Burke, as it happens, was referring
to a passage in *Paradise Lost*. But to the baroque poets Milton was *the*
master of the baroque Sublime.

point. The reader's mind is 'hurried out of itself' in the attempt, constantly made and regularly disappointed, to comprehend the poet's order, and the result is a 'crowd of great and confused images, which affect because they are crowded and confused'. The fact that its structure is apparently meaningless is the proof, to the reader, of the poem's sublimity. Its significance, if not rational, must be supra-rational, mystical, sublime.

Fundamentally therefore the baroque thrill is a psychological trick. An admiration for the apparent abruptness of the Old Testament and Pindar (with Milton their principal models) induced these poets to take a short cut to their sublimity. Their structure is not repetitive, like that of the Elizabethans, or organic like that of the metaphysicals, or logical, like that of the Augustans, but cumulative. It reduces itself ultimately to the catalogue. There is no internal connexion between the parts of the poem, which imposes itself by the sheer weight of its total effect.[1] The generalized images, the personifications and the sweep and grandeur of the abstractions

---

[1] A certain grammatical carelessness is symptomatic of the structural weakness. The first verse of Collins's 'Ode to Pity' for example: line 1, 'assign'd' performs a double duty (Pity, which is assigned the friend of man, is also assigned to bind his wounds); line 6, the 'unsated Foe', really Distress, seems to be either Pity or the object of Distress. Gray's 'The Descent of Odin' confuses the pronouns; in lines 5, 6, 'Him' and 'His' should both refer to Odin, but 'His' is actually the dog's; in line 13, 'he' (really Odin) should be the dog, the subject of the previous sentence. But the logic of grammar is not strictly applicable to the baroque style, which progresses by a sheer juxtaposition of images. (Its parallel is with the agglutinative languages, like Eskimo.)

*result* in a final impression of confused dignity which can be called sublimity. But the baroque sublime is a false sublime, because, like its diction, it is essentially artificial. Johnson's criticism of Gray's odes is applicable to the whole school:

> These odes are marked by glittering accumulations of ungraceful ornaments; they strike, rather than please; the images are magnified by affectation; the language is laboured into harshness. The mind of the writer seems to work with unnatural violence. ' Double, double, toil and trouble.' He has a kind of strutting dignity, and is tall by walking on tiptoe. His art and his struggle are too visible, and there is too little appearance of ease and nature.[1]

But though these poets fail, on the whole, to achieve ' sublimity ', they owe to their ambition a secondary success. Gray's ' Elegy ', Collins's ' Ode to Evening ', Akenside's ' Inscription for a Grotto ', and the best things in Thomson are not pure baroque, but they would not be what they are were it not for baroque influences. They have the baroque diction and they too tend to become catalogues. But instead of aiming at sublimity they are content to strike the lower note of the pastoral. And as it happens, whereas an artificial sublime must be a false sublime, the pastoral tradition is essentially a tradition of artifice. The sublimity of the baroque poets is *falsetto* because it is ' literary '—' by descriptions copied from descriptions, by imitations borrowed from imitations, by traditional imagery and hereditary similes '. But a pastoral cannot be

---

[1] 'Gray' (*Lives of the Poets*, 1781).

too ' literary '. Virgil's reminiscences of Theocritus, Spenser's of Mantuan, and Milton's of Fletcher and William Browne, are the very stuff out of which it is made. Its delicate landscapes and thin elfin music exactly suited the sensitive, learned, but half-hearted, Muses of Collins and Gray.

# IV

# THE NINETEENTH CENTURY

## I

THE baroque theory of language, the theory of 'poetic diction', was that poetry should possess, in Gray's words, 'a language peculiar to itself'. The functions of poetry and prose, it was maintained, are different, are even antithetical, and the further their words and word-order diverge the better each was likely to be. The Augustan position, on the other hand, was the opposite of this. Poetry, the Augustan would admit, is different from prose, it does not require *all* the words and idioms of prose, but the condition of its health and intelligibility is that those words that it does use—briefly, anything except archaisms, vulgarisms, and technical terms—shall derive from that common fund of language which it shares with prose. The two theories were therefore mutually contradictory. But, as it happens, though the baroque theory was often attacked by the later Augustans, especially by Johnson and Cowper, it was actually Wordsworth, a poet of quite another school, who finally discredited it.

The measure of the success of Wordsworth's devastating preface to the second edition of the *Lyrical Ballads* (1800) can be proved, as Coleridge noted, by 'the comparison of such poems of merit, as have been given to the public within the last ten or twelve years, with the majority of those produced previously to the appearance of that preface. Not only in the verses of those who have professsed their admiration of his genius, but even of those who have distinguished themselves by hostility to his theory, and depreciation of his writings, are the impressions of his principles plainly visible.'[1] The reason for Wordsworth's success I attribute to the fact that he opposed to the baroque theory a new and positive principle. Johnson's and Cowper's criticism was wholly negative and conservative. 'Gray', said Johnson, in a typical passage, ' thought his language more poetical as it was more remote from common use: finding in Dryden *honey redolent of spring*, an expression that reaches the utmost limits of our language, Gray drove it a little more beyond apprehension, by making *gales* to be *redolent of joy and youth* '.[2] But Johnson could only assert that Gray was wrong. He could recommend the avoidance of Gray's mistakes, but he had no new recipe of poetic beauty to substitute for them. Wordsworth, however, added to a diagnosis of the disease a prescription for its cure. ' The first Volume of these poems ', his preface begins, ' has already been submitted to general perusal. It was published, as an experiment, which, I hoped, might be of some use to ascertain, how far, by fitting to metrical arrangement a selection of the real language of men in a state of vivid sensation, that sort of pleasure and that quantity of pleasure may be imparted, which a Poet may rationally endeavour to impart.' Wordsworth was in agreement with Johnson, as far

---

[1] *Biographia Literaria*, 1817, ch. xvii.
[2] ' Gray ' (*Lives of the Poets*, 1781).

as Johnson went—'there neither is,' he wrote, 'nor can be, any *essential* difference between the language of prose and metrical composition'—but the novelty and the sting of his attack were in the rider he added—that the poet should employ a 'language really used by men'.

Wordsworth's preface cleared the air. But its influence on the new school of poetry that supplanted both the baroque poets and the later Augustans was indirect rather than direct. It had become unnecessary any longer, thanks to Wordsworth, to write either like Gray or like Pope, and in the relief of their release the poets forgot that they were now expected to write like a Cumberland peasant. Wordsworth forgot it himself. In neither his direct nor his grandiose manner is there a marked dependence, except in the weakest pieces, on 'language really used by men'. And Coleridge, Shelley, and Keats are even less dependent than Wordsworth. In other words, the style of the romantic poets, however it may be characterized, cannot possibly be described as colloquial. There is no need, however, to agree with Coleridge that Wordsworth's doctrine, 'in that degree in which it is practicable, yet as a rule it is useless, if not injurious, and therefore either need not, or ought not to be practised'.[1] A colloquial diction is not *a priori* unpoetical. The metaphysical poets used such a diction with brilliant success and in their most serious poems :

Since there's no help, come let us kiss and part. (*Drayton.*)

[1] *Biographia Literaria*, ch. xvii.

> I wonder, by my troth, what thou and I
> Did, till we loved ? (*Donne.*)

But whereas the colloquial diction of Drayton and Donne results, poetically, in an intensification, in Wordsworth's case it resulted in an enfeeblement. The diction dissipated the penetrating immediateness of effect at which he aimed, and which he achieved elsewhere with a non-colloquial diction; the simplicity, because it was too conscious, degenerated into a mawkish pseudo-simplicity, into *simplesse*. The only romantic poet who uses colloquial idioms with some measure of success is Byron :

> There's not a joy the world can give like that it takes
> away.
> O talk not to me of a name great in story.

But it is hardly necessary to point out how inferior, how much less *serious*, such lines are than Drayton's or Donne's. And Byron, in point of style, is the least romantic of all the romantic poets. His best critic, M. Charles du Bos, has rightly called the ' gift of *statement*, of bare, incisive enunciation, the Byronic gift par excellence '. ' Energy of expression —that is in my view the dominating factor in Byron's genius.' [1] But the gift of statement and energy of expression are the hall-marks not of romantic but of Augustan poetry.[2]

The theory of language implicit in the best poems of Wordsworth, Coleridge, Shelley, and Keats is not that of a ' language really used by men '. But neither

---

[1] *Byron and the Need of Fatality*, 1932.

[2] The Augustan style invited a measure of colloquialism. The popular idioms that Dryden used so successfully are an important element in

is it Coleridge's counter-theory that 'the language of a serious poem' requires 'an arrangement both of words and sentences, and a use and selection of (what are called) *figures of speech*, both as to their kind, their frequency, and their occasions, which on a subject of equal weight would be vicious and alien in correct and manly prose'.[1] Romantic diction does not exhibit a *conscious* deviation from the language of prose—such a deviation, for example, as characterizes the diction of Milton. It is impossible to say of the romantic poets either that they cultivate or that they avoid the diction of prose. They are apparently unaware of the distinction. They took their words where they could find them —from the spoken language, from the older poets, from their own invention (notably in Keats's case), even (as Professor J. L. Lowes has proved in his examination of 'The Ancient Mariner' and 'Kubla Khan') from books of travel. But this catholicity obscured a fundamental indifference. The problems of style and diction which had seemed so important to the eighteenth-century poets and critics had

the vigour of his verse. Consider, for example, the *Aeneis*, Book IX, lines 72–3 :

the bleating lambs
Securely swig the dug beside their dams.

The effect of an expression like ' swig the dug ' is to *reduce the interval* between the poet and his readers. They are men of the world together, who can look facts in the face and call them by their right names, the forcible, forbidden names of popular speech. But the footing on which Dryden and his readers meet is a social one. The romantic poet was not colloquial because he was anti-social, an individualist, an anarchist ; it was not to the vulgar surface of his readers' minds that he addressed himself, but to the recesses of their inner consciousness.

[1] *Biographia Literaria*, ch. xviii.

become almost irrelevant, certainly subordinate, to their nineteenth-century successors. 'It would seem', Newman summed up, 'that attention to the language *for its own sake* evidences not the true poet but the mere artist.'[1] And a similar ruling was adopted for the critics :

Among the systematic writers of modern times, from Scaliger downwards, criticism is almost wholly devoted to questions of language. They have studied figures of speech and varieties of metre, with little care for the weightier points of action, passion, manner, character, moral and intellectual aim. In simile and metaphor, in rhyme and rhythm, they have seen rules and measures, and they have reduced all the art of expression to a system as easy as grammar; but they have not sought to methodise the poet's dream, they have not cared in their analysis to grasp his higher thought.[2]

The principle that underlies the nineteenth-century bias against 'questions of language' was first enunciated by Carlyle. (It is implicit, however, in Wordsworth's preface and Shelley's *Defence of Poetry*.) 'Poetic creation,' Carlyle asks, in describing 'The Hero as Poet', 'what is this too but *seeing* the thing sufficiently ? The *word* that will describe the thing, follows of itself from such clear intense sight of the thing.' The dictum is an exact definition of the point of view of the romantic poets. It was their ambition to make poetry out of *things*. 'How little', Southey is made to say in one of Landor's *Imaginary Conversations*, 'hath been

---

[1] 'Poetry with Reference to Aristotle's Poetics', 1892. Quotation from reprint in E. D. Jones's *English Critical Essays (Nineteenth Century)*, 1916, p. 252.

[2] E. S. Dallas, *The Gay Science*, vol. 1, 1866, pp. 26–7.

objected against those who have substituted words for things, and how much against those who have re-instated things for words.' Wordsworth 'reinstated things for words'. 'I have at all times endeavoured,' he said, 'to look steadily at my subject.' It was the subject, the thing, that interested him, and the style that he tried to create was one that would re-flect his subjects with a minimum of distortion. Language, he told de Quincey, should not be 'the *dress* of thoughts' but 'the *incarnation* of thoughts', the thought itself made concrete.[1] And it is cer-tainly true that the reader is hardly conscious of the words in some of the best romantic poetry. Francis Thompson has noted the way in which Shelley's diction sometimes 'ceases to obtrude itself at all; it is imperceptible; his Muse has become a veritable Echo, whose body has dissolved from about her voice'.[2] And Matthew Arnold has made a similar claim, expressed equally fancifully, for Byron and Wordsworth. 'When he [Byron] warms to his work, when he is inspired, Nature herself seems to take the pen from him as she took it from Wordsworth, and to write for him as she wrote for Wordsworth, though in a different fashion, with her own pene-trating simplicity.'[3] We need not concern ourselves, for the moment, with the justice of Thompson's and Arnold's eulogies. It is romantic theory, not romantic practice, that I am anxious to isolate. But there is no doubt that Shelley and Wordsworth at

[1] Quoted in de Quincey's essay on 'Style'.
[2] *Shelley*, 1912, p. 66.
[3] 'Byron' (*Essays in Criticism, Second Series*).

any rate—of Byron I am not so sure—would have *liked* to be told that their Muses became Echos and that Nature seemed to take the pen from them. That was just the impression they intended to create.[1]

Carlyle's pronouncement that 'the *word* that will describe the thing, follows of itself' is reminiscent of Gascoigne's advice to the Elizabethan poets to concentrate 'upon some fine invention. For, that beyng founde, pleasant woordes will follow well inough'. And the similarity is not entirely accidental. The romantics evaded discussions of style for the same reason ultimately as the Elizabethans : a distrust of the language. But whereas the defect of Elizabethan English was that it was too fluid, the defect of the English of the early nineteenth century, from the point of view of the romantic poets, was that it was too rigid. The long process of discipline to which the language had been submitted by the Royal Society and Locke and their

---

[1] Keats, decidedly the most *language-conscious* of romantic poets, began by adopting a position similar to Wordsworth's : 'Poetry should be great and unobtrusive, a thing which enters into one's soul, and does not startle it or amaze it with itself, but with its subject' (*Letters*, edited by M. Buxton Forman, vol. i, p. 103). Later, however, he changed his ground :

> Poesy alone can tell her dreams,
> With the fine spell of words alone can save
> Imagination from the sable chain
> And dumb enchantment. Who alive can say,
> ' Thou art no Poet—may'st not tell thy dreams ? '
> Since every man whose soul is not a clod
> Hath visions, and would speak, if he had loved,
> And been well nurtured in his mother tongue.
>
> (*The Fall of Hyperion*, ll. 8–15.)

followers in the eighteenth century, and which had culminated in the elaborate codification of Johnson's Dictionary, had left English an instrument of remarkable efficiency—for certain purposes. The dialogue in the novels of Jane Austen and Peacock could not be improved upon for exactness and clarity, and the prose of Landor's *Imaginary Conversations* is equally, though differently, precise. But exactness of denotation and clarity of progression were qualities that only embarassed the romantic poet. They were positive impediments to the expression of the subliminal excitements he exploited. The language that had been evolved through the eighteenth century was a language of the surface. Its words had been restricted to their first, immediate meanings and had lost the sub-intentions, the *aura* of circumambient suggestion, that poetry normally requires. And the romantic poets found that these words betrayed their intentions. Wordsworth's admission is significant—' my language may frequently have suffered from those arbitrary connexions of feelings and ideas with particular words and phrases, from which no man can altogether protect himself. Hence I have no doubt, that, in some instances, feelings, even of the ludicrous, may be given to my Readers by expressions which appeared to me tender and pathetic.' [1] But the trouble went deeper than Wordsworth realized. No doubt some words and idioms proved more unmanageable than others, but *every* word, *every* idiom that the eighteenth century had trimmed and tamed was

[1] 'Preface' (*Lyrical Ballads*, 1800).

potentially treacherous. They had been 'treated' for non-romantic purposes and were simply not adequate, without violence, to the expression of shades of meaning outside the field originally contemplated for them.

I am inclined to attribute to this fact a characteristic defect of romantic poetry. I mean the lapses and inconsistencies of style that disfigure all but the best poems of Wordsworth, Coleridge, Byron, Shelley, and Keats. There is nothing comparable to these lapses in the poetry of other periods. Spenser can be dull, but even the dullest lines in *The Faerie Queene* are always unmistakably Spenser's; Swinburne can be vapid, but his vapidity can never be confused with that of another poet. But the worst passages of the romantic poets might be by any one. They are completely without the individual stamp that later and earlier poets, naturally far less richly endowed, impress upon their work. The style of the romantic poets is uncertain and quite without the ease, the inevitability and the assurance that mark the master of language. They were never, indeed, absolute masters of the English language. To some extent they may be said to have imposed themselves upon it and to have carved out of it an individual idiom. But their hold was always precarious. There was always a danger that the language would betray them. It is not without significance that 'The Ancient Mariner' and 'La Belle Dame sans Merci', the two quite flawless romantic poems,[1] being ballads, are in a style and

---

[1] Coventry Patmore, no bad judge, once pronounced 'La Belle Dame

diction almost uncontaminated by eighteenth-century influences.

The uncertainty of the diction of the romantic poets was their misfortune. It was not their fault that the words they were compelled to use had been whittled down to the purity of mathematical symbols. But the slovenliness of style, the hit-or-miss quality, of the great bulk of romantic poetry is another matter. Professor de Selincourt has recently published a fragment of Wordsworth's which contains a curious admission :

> I burst forth
> In verse which, with a strong and random light
> Touching an object in its prominent parts,
> Created a memorial which to me
> Was all sufficient, and to my own mind
> Recalling the whole picture, seemed to speak
> An universal language. Scattering thus
> In passion many a desultory sound,
> I deemed that I had adequately clothed
> Meanings at which I hardly hinted, thought
> And forms of which I scarcely had produced
> An arbitrary sign.[1]

Wordsworth's lines are a confession of the central defect not only of his own poetry, but of too much of Coleridge's, Byron's, and Shelley's, and even (in *Endymion*) of Keats's. Romantic poetry, instead of being the exact expression of the originating intention, tends to be an approximation only. The

sans Merci ' ' probably the very finest lyric in the English language ' (*Principle in Art*, 1890, p. 81).

[1] I quote from Professor de Selincourt's lecture *On Poetry*, 1929, p. 15.

outlines are blurred ; the emotion is diffused ; the argument wavers. And the defect can fairly be called central because it is a corollary of the romantic doctrine of *inspiration*. The definitions of poetry that the romantic poets have let fall—'all good poetry is the spontaneous overflow of powerful feelings',[1] 'poetry is the lava of the imagination, whose eruption prevents an earthquake',[2] 'poetry is not subject to the control of the active powers of the mind, and its birth and recurrence have no necessary connexion with the consciousness or will',[3] ' if Poetry comes not as naturally as the Leaves to a tree it had better not come at all '[4]—are agreed in the importance they assign to its spontaneity. Poetry is automatic. The 'word that will describe the thing' follows *of itself*. They emphasize, that is, the part played in the poetic act by the subconscious mind and they minimize the importance of the conscious activities of control and discrimination. The spirit of poetry has but to breathe through the inspired man, or the ' genius ' (as the romantics called him), and the masterpiece dictates itself. But, as Mr. Logan Pearsall Smith has pointed out, ' the word genius implies the permanent possession of magical power ; and all the works of a genius, being regarded as the products of this power, are accepted in a spirit cf worship and without discrimination. Thus criticism is blurred, and the

[1] Wordsworth, 'Preface' (*Lyrical Ballads*, 1800).
[2] Byron, *Letters and Journals*, ed. R. E. Prothero, vol. iii, 1900, p. 405.
[3] Shelley, *A Defence of Poetry*, 1821.
[4] Keats, *Letters*, ed. M. B. Forman, vol. i, 1931, p. 116.

genius himself, believing in the unfailing potency of his gift, tends to work in a slovenly manner.' [1]

## II

If one compares, as one fairly may from the similarity of the matter, the diction of Thackeray's novels with Fielding's, or Dickens's with Sterne's, a fact of some interest emerges. Fielding and Sterne are quite as sentimental as Thackeray and Dickens, but the emotions that their novels communicate are one remove farther away. The emotions are released by the situations; they lie *behind* the words. The emotions of Dickens and Thackeray, on the other hand, are rawer and more exposed. They *adhere* to the words, which provide an emotional accompaniment to the situations.

The difference is the measure of the change which the English language had undergone in the century dividing the four novelists. In 1750 the tendency was for words to be purely denotative— to be restricted, that is, to their primary and 'official' meanings. It was the tribute exacted from the language by the intellectualism of the age. But with the coming of the nineteenth century, with the coming not only of the romantic movement in poetry but of the hundred other movements in life and thought that went to make up the Victorian complex, the rigidity of the language relaxed. The emotions, no longer compelled to hide behind an intellectual structure, began to express themselves directly, and the connotations of words gradually

[1] *Four Words*, S.P.E., 1924, p. 40.

came to seem as important as, and sometimes more important than, their denotations. Precision of statement was less necessary; suggestiveness and 'atmosphere' had taken its place.

The new models of style were the Elizabethan and Jacobean writers. ('From the common opinion', said Coleridge, 'that the English style attained its greatest perfection in and about Queen Anne's reign I altogether dissent.')[1] Byron, with his keen eye for an affectation, ridiculed the change of fashion. He was 'told that the new school were to revive the language of Queen Elizabeth, the true English : as every body in the reign of Queen Anne wrote no better than French, by a species of literary treason'.[2] And it is true there was an element of artificiality in the revival. For the language of the early nineteenth century is really quite different from that of the early seventeenth century. Both periods may be said to have sacrificed denotation to connotation, but it was to two different kinds of connotation. In the metaphysical period the connotation of a word *grew* out of its denotation—the two are so entangled that it is impossible to know where one begins and the other ends. But the connotation of a nineteenth-century word was *superimposed* upon its denotation—the denotation it had possessed in the eighteenth century—and the two meanings exist separately and, as it were, side by side. It was possible, that is, given the appropriate context, to employ a word either for its denotation

[1] 'On Style' (*Essays and Lectures*).
[2] *Letters and Journals*, ed. R. E. Prothero, vol. iv, 1900, p. 490.

alone or for its connotation alone. But the enhanced significance of Jacobean diction, the resonance that gave it its prestige with the Victorians, depends precisely upon the impossibility of separating what a word denotes from what it connotes. (It is the grand secret of the prose of the Authorized Version of the Bible.) Jacobean diction is both precise and profound. The best mid-Victorian diction, on the other hand, though sometimes precise (Mill is precise, Bagehot is precise) and sometimes profound ('a network of tentacular roots reaching down to the deepest terrors and desires'), rarely if ever unites the two qualities either in its prose or its poetry. The Victorians spoke two languages, reflecting the divided aims and origins of their civilization : a language of the heart, and a language of the head. It is not necessary to call this hypocrisy (they were the victims of irresistible tendencies), but poetically the bifurcation was a disaster.

A modern historian has noted as a peculiar characteristic of nineteenth-century political thought the 'multiplicity of elements unabsorbed into a common thing'.[1] The lines of thought are parallel and never meet. But Victorianism is more easily defined in terms of its feelings than of its thoughts. A Victorian who thought at all was bound apparently to think differently from everybody else. The rival systems of Carlyle, Mill, Ruskin, Spencer, Newman, and Arnold are such poles apart that they scarcely even contradict each other. It is only in

[1] Crane Brinton, *English Political Thought in the Nineteenth Century*, 1933, p. 293.

feeling that they are comparable. There, however, their limitations and excesses are curiously the same. The emotional centre of Victorianism, as I see it, is conveniently indicated in a remark attributed to Tennyson : 'the evils he denounces are individual, only to be cured by each man looking to his own heart'.[1] The evils the Victorians denounced were always individual, and the 'heart', the conscience, was always their cure. (The conscience is the real hero not only of the novels of rationalists like George Eliot but also of such a work as Newman's *Grammar of Assent*.) Dallas, one of the best of the Victorian critics, commented on Tennyson's line,

The individual withers, and the world is more and more :

But I am not sure whether the essence of this thought might not be expressed in the very opposite terms : the in-dividual prospers, and the world is less and less. The great point to be seized is that there is gradually being wrought a change in the relation of the individual to the mass. Whether we regard that change as a growth or as a withering will depend very much on what we think of the indi-vidual. If the individual in whom we are most interested is what is generally understood by a hero, then certainly it must be confessed that he withers. The little men and the private men and all the incidents of privacy are coming into repute. We dwell far more than we used to do on the private side of human life. Now the private virtues are be-coming public, and the private life is rising into public importance.[2]

But the acclamations and accusations of the private conscience, if intense and profound, are necessarily

[1] *Tennyson. A Memoir. By his Son*, vol. i, 1897, p. 468.
[2] *The Gay Science*, vol. ii, 1866, p. 280.

vague. They elude words. A feeling of moral
rapture or remorse can only be translated into adequate words with the help of just such an organized
religion or philosophical system as the Victorians
were unable to provide. And since such feelings
must be expressed at all costs it was the words that
suffered. The diction became as vague and diffuse
as the emotions.

The pioneers of the English romantic movement
—Wordsworth, Coleridge, and Southey—had been
handicapped by the uncongeniality of the language
they found in use. The second generation of romantic poets (Tennyson, Browning, Mrs. Browning,
FitzGerald, and Arnold) were more fortunate in
possessing a language that suited them. It was
easier for them to write. Their poems do not suffer
from the lapses and inconsistencies of style that disfigure the earlier poets. But, though it was easier
for Tennyson and Arnold to write well, it was next
to impossible for them to write supremely well. The
language with which Wordsworth and Coleridge
had wrestled and which they had sometimes succeeded in compelling to their purposes, was excellent
of its kind, though it was not their kind—a tyrant,
but a tyrant worthy of their daggers. The necessity
under which they lay of resisting the linguistic
tendencies of the previous century was itself a
stimulus. But the language that Tennyson found
to his hands was a flabby and submissive thing. He
did what he could with it ; he was a natural stylist,
with an inborn interest and instinct for words.[1] And

---

[1] His casual comments prove it : ' Wordsworth seemed to him *thick-*

yet, with all his critical awareness, with all his charm and fluency, what a poor thing relatively Tennyson's style is! Slow, monotonous, overcoloured, over-musical, its essential diffuseness only emphasized by the niggling detail. 'A poet', Coleridge has observed, 'ought not to pick nature's pocket : let him borrow, and so borrow as to repay by the very act of borrowing. Examine nature accurately, but write from recollection ; and trust more to your imagination than to your memory.'[1] Tennyson trusted more to his memory than to his imagination, and more to his note-books than to his memory. But this fussy accuracy of his, distracting though it is, was in a way praiseworthy. It was Tennyson's protest against the vagueness, the emotional mist, in which the diction of Victorian poetry was wrapped. The style to which he naturally tended was, I believe, something cooler and more concentrated than the condition of the language ever permitted him to achieve :

> You'll have no scandal while you dine,
> But honest talk and wholesome wine,
>     And only hear the magpie gossip
> Garrulous under a roof of pine ;
>
> For groves of pine on either hand,
> To break the blast of winter, stand ;
>     And further on, the hoary Channel
> Tumbles a billow on chalk and sand.

*ankled*' ; ' I can't read Ben Jonson, especially his comedies. To me he appears to move in a wide sea of glue' (*Tennyson. A Memoir. By his Son*, vol. ii, 1897, pp. 505, 205), two judgements that could not be improved upon.

[1] *Specimens of the Table-Talk*, vol. i, 1835, p. 208.

I seem to detect in these lines to F. D. Maurice, as at moments in 'The Palace of Art' and 'In Memoriam', a distant hint, a tantalizing premonition, of a poetry of the might-have-been in which a Horace collaborates with a Marvell.

But, with all the deductions made that must be made, Tennyson did obtain a minor success. The style that he elaborated was as economical and as precise as the language permitted. Its virtue is its consistency, and it was a consistent style because it was a conscious style. The peculiarities of Victorian English had been taken into account, its merits had been made the most of, its vicious propensities had been partially discounted. Tennyson did not try to write either in ignorance of or in indifference to the linguistic tendencies of his time. His poems are made out of the diction of the day—'the best words in the best order' that were then available, and his limited success serves to show up the failure of the other romantic poets of his generation. Tennyson was at least aware of the condition of the language he was compelled to use. His contemporaries, on the contrary, were *language-proof*. They bluntly refused to concern themselves with problems of diction and style. 'The poet', they would have agreed with Newman, 'is a compositor; words are his types; he must have them within reach, and in unlimited abundance.'[1] And the consequence of this mechanical conception of composition was that, falling unconscious victims to the contradictory tendencies of the period, they cannot strictly be said

[1] Op. cit., p. 251.

to have a *style* at all. They have idiosyncrasies of expression ; but that is another matter.

A theory of poetry that has no place for diction must offer something in its stead. The Victorians offered the subject. The romantic ideal of style was, as we have seen, 'something which must derive its poetic validity entirely from the matter committed to it'.[1] The earlier romantic poets had derived this matter from the subconscious mind. If they selected one subject rather than another, it was because some subjects will stimulate the subconscious mind more than others. They had not fallen into the mistake, into which the later poets fell, of considering some subjects essentially poetical. 'A great artist', Byron once said, 'will make a block of stone as sublime as a mountain, and a good poet can imbue a pack of cards with more poetry than inhabits the forests of America.'[2] With this dictum we may contrast Matthew Arnold's war-cry : 'All depends upon the subject ; choose a fitting action, penetrate yourself with the feeling of its situations ; this done, everything else will follow.'[3] The subject was the red herring of Victorian criticism, and many of the errors of that criticism—its neglect of Donne, its half-heartedness to Blake, its disparagement of Shelley[4]—are directly traceable to its influence. But it would be incorrect to attribute all

[1] I have borrowed this excellent definition from Professor Lascelles Abercrombie's *Romanticism*, 1926, p. 25.

[2] *Letters and Journals*, ed. R. E. Prothero, vol. v, 1901, p. 557.

[3] 'Preface' (*Poems*, 1853).

[4] Palgrave's *Golden Treasury* omits Donne and Blake altogether. Arnold ('Byron' in *Essays in Criticism. Second Series*) detected in

the deficiencies of the Victorian poets to the doctrine of the subject. The most that can be said is that it encouraged them in their habits of linguistic indifference. The real case against mid-Victorian poetry, other than Tennyson's, is not that it rests upon a mistaken basis of theory but that it is badly written.

The example of Matthew Arnold is especially instructive because Arnold was not naturally a poet but a man of letters. His place is with such writers as Addison and Goldsmith, and Mr. Aldous Huxley to-day—writers who, one feels, at whatever period they happen to be born, *must* express themselves through literature, though the particular literary form they may select is ultimately immaterial and dependent on the fashion of the moment. Poetry happened to possess more prestige than any other form in the mid-ninteenth century, and Arnold wrote poems. But I can find no trace in all his intelligent and readable verse of any specifically poetic originality. The sensibility reflected in it is not that of Arnold himself but of his age, and the style is an amalgam of the language that was then available for poetry. And what language it was !

> And Wordsworth ! Ah, pale Ghosts, rejoice !
> For never has such soothing voice
> Been to your shadowy world convey'd,
> Since erst, at morn, some wandering shade
> Heard the clear song of Orpheus come
> Through Hades, and the mournful gloom.

Shelley ' the incurable want of a sound subject-matter '—an opinion shared by Patmore (*Principle in Art*, 1890, p. 114).

Apart from the vicious exclamations—a p trick of Arnold's, like the forcible-feeble use of italics, and both traceable to a desperate effort to impart an artificial emphasis to a naturally unemphatic diction—was it necessary to describe *Ghosts* as *pale*? If Hades is populated by wandering *shades* need we be told that it is *shadowy*? Is not *gloom* always *mournful*? And logical confusion is added to the redundancy. Wordsworth's *soothing* voice is compared to Orpheus's *clear* song. But why, especially in the gloom of Hades, should a clear song be soothing? One would have imagined that it would be more likely to be disturbing. What finally is the significance of *at morn*? Is not Hades always equally dark? Or, if there are gradations of light, are we to visualize the relative darkness or the relative brightness of morning?

The passage I have quoted is not in the least exceptional. Read hurriedly it is not unimpressive. But once it is subjected to a critical scrutiny the vagueness of its diction and the looseness of its thought are inescapable. The words are the ghosts of words. Two words have to be used to do the work of one. And the trickle of meaning is obscured in a fog of associations conjured up by the implied reference to parallel passages in the *Odyssey*, the *Georgics*, and the *Aeneid*. It would be unfair, however, to lay all the blame on Arnold, who merely accepted the style and the language current in his time. It is the limitations of that style and that language, especially in conjunction, that I wish to emphasize. Arnold's style is clear, his diction diffuse. There were therefore two alternatives that he evaded : he could either have clarified his diction, as Tennyson to some extent did ; or, like the Pre-Raphaelites, he could have diffused his style.

## III

' Poetry, in our day ', Landor wrote in the laconic preface to the 1859 edition of *The Hellenics*, 'is oftener prismatic than diaphanous : this is not so : they who look into it may see through.' It was a concise definition of the central difference between Landor's own style (which approximates to that of such mid-eighteenth-century writers as Akenside) and that of the Victorian poets. Landor is transparent ; the Victorians are opaque. But the definition, in 1859, was more relevant to the poetry of the immediate future than to that of the immediate past. Matthew Arnold, the bulk of whose verse was published between 1849 and 1857, certainly wrote in a style that it was impossible, for those who looked into it, to see through. But was it *prismatic*? The word describes far better, not Arnold's neutral tones, but the iridescent poetry of the Pre-Raphaelites. ' The Blessed Damozel' *is* prismatic. And so are ' Goblin Market ', ' The Life and Death of Jason', and ' Atalanta in Calydon '. But, with the exception of ' The Blessed Damozel ' (first published in *The Germ* in 1850), these poems date from the years 1862–7.

The distinction of the Pre-Raphaelites, Rossetti's and Swinburne's in particular, was to have brought back into Victorian poetry a love of words for their own sake. Rossetti 'collected' words. 'I have done but little in any way,' he wrote to his brother in 1849, 'having wasted several days at the Museum, where I have been reading up all manner of old romaunts, to pitch upon stunning words for poetry. I have found several.'[1] The finds are scattered through his poems—'grame', 'dole', 'grout', 'teen', &c. No one probably would claim now that Rossetti's 'stunners' helped his poetry. They are symptomatic, indeed, of the irresponsibility that accompanied his enthusiasm. (A word was 'stunning' often only because it was out-of-the-way.) But the mistake was a fault on the right side in 1849. Rossetti's verbal excesses were tonic just because they were verbal. To the pundits who thundered—Matthew Arnold among them— 'Choose better subjects,' Rossetti retorted 'Choose better words'. The two slogans may have been both unduly simplified, but Rossetti's was at least the more practical and the more heartening. The early Victorians had tried all sorts of subjects with very little success ; they had not tried all sorts of words.

Tennyson is a partial exception to this generalization. But Tennyson, though decidedly a better poet than most of the Pre-Raphaelites, did not exert a comparable influence on the younger writers. His style—that is, the *direction* of his style —was opposed to the linguistic tendencies of the nineteenth century. The Rossettis and Swinburne, on the other hand, were in full sympathy with those

[1] *Family Letters*, vol. ii, 1895, p. 51.

tendencies. They encouraged and exploited them. The vagueness and diffuseness of Victorian English, only a nuisance to Tennyson, were admirably adapted to express the dreamlike quality of their vision :

> A little while a little love
> > The hour yet bears for thee and me.     (*Rossetti.*)
>
> Not a lily on the land,
> > Or lily on the water.     (*Christina Rossetti.*)
>
> I heard all night and all the hours of it.
> > > (*Swinburne.*)

The diffuseness of such phrases is different from the diffuseness of 'In Memoriam' or Arnold's poems. It is a paraded diffuseness, deliberate and ostentatious. The Pre-Raphaelites *tried* to be diffuse. The secret of their influence is that they fitted to the blurred meanings and dim associations of Victorian diction a mode of apprehension and a style that were equally blurred and dim. They wrote *with* the language, whereas Tennyson, Arnold, and the Brownings (in their several degrees of more or less) wrote *against* it, and their reward is the inevitability—'the carol, the creation'—that sets Swinburne at any rate in the same class as a Spenser, a Donne, and a Dryden. The 'Atalanta' choruses, 'The Triumph of Time', and the poem on Baudelaire ('Ave atque Vale'), to name no others, are perfect of their kind—though one may not like the kind. Tennyson's poetry, on the other hand, is never absolutely perfect (Keats would always have done it rather better), though as a kind it is natural to prefer it.

The diffuseness of Victorian English was ultimately derived from a loosening of the connexion between the connotations and the denotations of words. The two meanings, as we have seen, had come to exist almost independently, with a mutual loss of vividness and precision. A word had its normal meaning, its 'dictionary' meaning, and, side by side with that, a secondary meaning created by the contexts in which it was used. The difficulty therefore for the hearer or reader on each occasion was to be certain which meaning was intended—or rather, how *much* of each meaning, the proportion of primary and secondary meaning being constantly variable. And it was just the indecision in which this condition tended to terminate—in other words, the feeling of *vagueness*—that the Pre-Raphaelites exploited. Swinburne's words are vague because he has included all their meanings, primary and secondary, impartially. It is impossible to know which aspect of a word, which centre of meaning, he wished to emphasize. But the impossibility is the point. The incongruousness that the reader experiences, the difficulty of connecting up the juxtaposed implications of the diction, leads to precisely that surrender of the logical faculty, with the consequent feeling of revelation, that the Pre-Raphaelite style requires.

> Before the beginning of years
>     There came to the making of man
> Time with a gift of tears ;
>     Grief with a glass that ran.

'The chorus of Swinburne', Mr. T. S. Eliot

remarks, ' is almost a parody of the Athenian : it is
sententious but it has not even the significance of a
commonplace . . . it is effective because it appears
to be a tremendous statement, like statements made
in dreams ; when we wake up we find that the
' glass that ran ' would do better for time than
for grief, and that the gift of tears would be as
appropriately bestowed by grief as by time '.[1] But
the objection is irrelevant. The Pre-Raphaelites do
not deal in revelations but in the *feeling* of revelation. There are no statements, in the ordinary sense,
in their poems at all. What they communicate, with
untiring artistry and superb *élan*, is a state of mind
—the state of mind of a dreamer. The value of that
state of mind is, of course, another question.

The detail that is an occasional characteristic of
Pre-Raphaelite verse and the air of unnecessary
precision that accompanies it, have the effect para-
doxically of accentuating the prevalent vagueness.
The numbers that Rossetti and Swinburne delight
in are an example of this :

> She had three lilies in her hand,
> > And the stars in her hair were seven.    (*Rossetti.*)
>
> There were four apples on the bough.    (*Swinburne.*)

Why *three* lilies, *seven* stars, *four* apples ? The
reader concludes that the numbers must be important because they are specified so carefully. But
they are not important. What Swinburne and
Rossetti were interested in was not the exact number
of the lilies, stars, or apples, but the feeling of

---

[1] *The Sacred Wood*, 1920, p. 135.

exactness those numbers convey. Rossetti has described the Pre-Raphaelite ideal as 'the constant unison of wonder and familiarity so mysteriously allied in nature, the sense of fulness and abundance such as we feel in a field, not because we pry into it all, but because it is all there'.[1] It is an excellent definition. Pre-Raphaelite poetry, like the world of dreams, is both strange and familiar. But the technical basis of this 'constant unison of wonder and familiarity' is, on the one hand, an abuse of language, and, on the other hand, an abuse of detail.

[1] *Collected Works*, vol. i, 1901, p. 444. Rossetti's abuse of numbers may have been encouraged by the 'kisses four' of 'La Belle Dame sans Merci' (one of his favourite poems). Keats deleted the phrase in the final draft of the poem.

# V

# THE PRESENT DAY

## I

'SWINBURNE was a tremendous force in poetry: the force died; the man outlived it, and died, many years later, solicitously tended.' That, in the opinion of Sir Arthur Quiller-Couch,[1] is what constitutes Swinburne's tragedy. But the tragedy is really not the tragedy of Swinburne but of Pre-Raphaelite poetry. Pre-Raphaelite poetry was a force for only twenty years—from 1858 (the year in which Morris's *Defence of Guinevere* was published) to 1878 (the date of Swinburne's *Poems and Ballads, Second Series*). It is true that Morris, Swinburne, Christina Rossetti, and the army of their imitators went on writing Pre-Raphaelite poems—they are still being written to-day—but, to quote Sir Arthur Quiller-Couch again, 'none of them mattered, none of them contained any longer any hope; all were galvanic—reflex action of genius after death'.

Criticism has been too apt to explain this phenomenon in terms of the individual Pre-Raphaelites. And no doubt Watts-Dunton's marching off of Swinburne to Putney in 1879 *did* make a difference —to Swinburne. No doubt Christina Rossetti's refusal to marry Charles Bagot Cayley had something to do with *her* ossification. But the difference is a general difference, the ossification a universal ossification. Pre-Raphaelite poetry ceased to have

[1] *Studies in Literature,* 1919, p. 250.

any real significance after 1880 (with an exception to be noted presently) not because of the failure of this or that poet but because of a change in the condition of the language. It had been made possible by the vagueness of mid-Victorian English; its function disappeared when the language became precise again.

The deliquescence of the language had attained its maximum in or about 1860, and in the later years of the century a contrary process, a process of crystallization, set in. It was a reaction similar to that inaugurated in the seventeenth century by the Royal Society. The connotation of words, as then, had tended to obliterate their denotation and the language had become loose, unwieldy, and verbose.[1] A more flexible and precise diction was a necessity. But the change of direction, a matter of intensive propaganda in the seventeenth century, was accomplished in the nineteenth century almost unseen and, as it were, unintentionally. The fact of a change is obvious, but the motives prompting and perpetrating it can only be guessed at. We may plausibly attribute it, however, as in the seventeenth century, to the working of the scientific spirit. The rationalism that has gradually penetrated into every recess of modern thought cannot but have influenced the

---

[1] Alice Meynell, one of the new precisians, condemned the 'exaggeration' of the Pre-Raphaelites : 'we resent exaggeration if we care for our English language. For exaggeration writes relaxed, and not elastic, words and verses ; and it is possible that the language suffers something, at least temporarily—during the life of a couple of generations, let us say—from the loss of elasticity brought about by such a strain' ('Dickens as a Man of Letters' in *Hearts of Controversy*, 1917).

Line 7. *For* precise again *read* more precise again

medium of that thought, and the natural direction of its influence must have been towards clarity.

The immediate effect on Pre-Raphaelite poetry of the new tendency towards a greater precision of language was to restrict its diction. The vagueness upon which it flourished, though it had left the living language, still adhered to the words and phrases that the earlier romantic poets had consecrated. And so there rose that 'poetic diction' that Francis Thompson assailed in a famous passage of his essay on Shelley:

Poetic diction has become latterly a kaleidoscope, and one's chief curiosity is as to the precise combinations into which the pieces will be shifted. There is, in fact, a certain band of words, the Praetorian cohorts of poetry, whose prescriptive aid is invoked by every aspirant to the poetical purple; against them it is time some banner should be raised. Perhaps it is almost impossible for a contemporary writer quite to evade the services of the free-lances whom one encounters under so many standards. But it is at any rate curious to note that the literary revolution against the despotic diction of Pope seems issuing, like political revolutions, in a despotism of its own making.[1]

The best of the later Pre-Raphaelites—Flecker, Rupert Brooke, and Mr. de la Mare—have given

---

[1] *Shelley*, 1912, pp. 25–6. The essay was written in 1889. Curiously enough Watts-Dunton, the critic *en titre* of the Pre-Raphaelites, has the same criticism to make: 'a new kind of poetic diction now grew up—a diction composed mainly of that of Shelley and of Keats, of Tennyson, of Rossetti, of Swinburne, yet mixed with Elizabethan and more archaic forms—a diction, to be sure, far more poetic in its elements than that which Coleridge, Scott, and Wordsworth did so much to abolish, but none the less artificial' (*Poetry and the Renascence of Wonder*, ed. T. Hake, 1916, p. 296).

this diction a moment more of life, but it has only been by something that is almost equivalent to parody. They have carried off its artificiality by half-laughing at it:

> These I have loved:
>   White plates and cups, clean-gleaming,
> Ringed with blue lines; and feathery, faery dust;
> Wet roofs, beneath the lamp-light; the strong crust
> Of friendly bread; and many-tasting food.

The effectiveness of Brooke's 'The Great Lover' (from which these lines come), as in their different ways of Flecker's 'Old Ships' and Mr. de la Mare's 'The Tryst',[1] depends ultimately, apart from occasional felicities of phrasing, upon the impudent incongruousness of the matter with the manner. The manner announces Pre-Raphaelite generalities; the matter turns out to be a precise and realistic catalogue. But incongruousness of this kind, which is similar to that exploited by writers of burlesques and mock-heroics, is not really a kind of poetry but a kind of humour. The case for Brooke as a humorist is a strong one; the poet, when deserted by the humourist (as in many of the sonnets), is inconsiderable, a mere retailer of Pre-Raphaelite commonplaces. Brooke had accepted the Pre-Raphaelite idiom because it was the only idiom available when he began to write, but instead of discarding it on discovering its incompatibility with

---

[1] His best poem in the opinion of a judicious admirer, Mr. J. Middleton Murry.

the language he was speaking and working out—like Gerard Manley Hopkins and Mr. A. E. Housman—an idiom of his own, Brooke had preferred to put the old diction, with brilliant success, to a new, if rather unworthy, use.

Brooke's success is less interesting therefore than the failures, comparatively speaking, of Hopkins and Mr. Housman. Hopkins's abortive revolt against the Pre-Raphaelite tradition goes back to the year 1876 (the date of 'The Wreck of the Deutschland'), and that it was abortive I attribute primarily to that fact. Hopkins was too early. The language had not increased sufficiently in precision by then for the massive concrete poetry of Hopkins to be possible at all without very special precautions. The clumsy, and, as one feels now, unnecessary, concentration of his style was in fact necessary in 1876. Without the restriction it imposed the tendencies of the language would have carried him away into the vagueness and diffuseness that he was in revolt against. The danger is apparent in his earlier poems, even in the magnificent 'Heaven-Haven' (written about 1866):

> And I have asked to be
>   Where no storms come,
> Where the green swell is in the havens dumb,
>   And out of the swing of the sea.

To his contemporaries Hopkins's lines may well have seemed much the same thing as Christina Rossetti's 'Spring Quiet' (also written about 1866):

Here the sun shineth
Most shadily;
Here is heard an echo
Of the far sea,
Though far off it be.

The two poems are essentially at opposite poles, Christina Rossetti's representing an escape from and Hopkins's a confrontation of reality, but the condition of the language had tended to assimilate them. Mr. A. E. Housman, coming twenty years later, was able to benefit by the language's gains of precision in the interval; *A Shropshire Lad* has exactly those qualities of directness, concision, and inevitability that Hopkins's style just misses. But Mr. Housman, though he has had imitators, has not founded a school. There is a fatal flaw in his verse, the flaw of *insincerity*, that all its brilliance of detail cannot quite obscure. The fact is, I believe, that if Hopkins was premature, Mr. Housman came too late. *A Shropshire Lad*, stylistically Georgian, is temperamentally mid-Victorian.

Ay, look: high heaven and earth ail from the prime
    foundation;
All thoughts to rive the heart are here, and all are vain:
Horror and scorn and hate and fear and indignation—
    Oh why did I awake? when shall I sleep again?

Mr. Housman's *taedium vitae* would have been more appropriately expressed in an earlier and more diffuse idiom—FitzGerald's for example, or Swinburne's. The style, as it is, is too precise for the emotion. It *distorts* it, and a distorted emotion is an insincere emotion.

The historical significance of Hopkins and Mr. Housman is in the sphere of diction. The tendency of Victorian poetry had been to reduce little by little the number of living words and to substitute for them the Praetorian cohorts of romantic poetic diction. Hopkins and Mr. Housman—assisted by Robert Bridges, Charles Doughty, and Thomas Hardy—rebelled against this tendency. Their efforts were tentative and sometimes mistaken— they exaggerated the value of archaisms and dialectal words and phrases; but they initiated a process that has culminated in the one indisputable achievement of post-War poetry—its catholicity of diction.

A poetry that is coextensive with the language in which it is written has always been extremely rare. Dryden was the last English poet whose verse has even approached such a condition. But we are on the verge of such a poetry at this moment. The signs and portents are all around us. Mr. Stephen Spender, for example, one of the youngest of contemporary poets, is now able to begin a poem, and a fine poem, in this way:

> Passing, men are sorry for the birds in cages
> And for constricted nature hedged and lined;
> But what do they say to your pleasant bird
> Physical delight, since years tamed?
>
> Behind centuries, behind the continual hill,
> The wood you felled, your clothes, the slums you built,
> Only love knows where that bird dips his head;
> Only the sun, soaked in memory, flashes on his neck.

The remarkable thing here is the success with which

Mr. Spender conciliates words with such diverse and conflicting areas of suggestion as *constricted*, *physical*, *slums*, and *love*. And the words do not force themselves upon the reader; they are right and inevitable. A romantic poet, faced with the same subject, would have been compelled to take refuge in the contorted periphrases that Tennyson was often driven to.

The problem of diction has been simplified for the modern poet by the fact that we are much less sensitive to the connotations of words than our fathers and grandfathers were. A word is taken more at its face-value nowadays. It is not so liable to explode if brought into contact with words of which the associations are different. But the language, if less explosive, is also less emphatic than it was, and it is this lack of emphasis, this hesitancy, that is the characteristic defect of contemporary poetry. A modern poet wears an air of self-conscious casuality. He seems to be thinking aloud; his poems have the abruptness and untidiness of thought in the raw. And, as a result of this underemphasis, he is unable either to *impose* himself, like a classical poet, or to *insinuate* himself, like a romantic poet. There is a danger that he may not make himself heard.

Wilfred Owen is the one modern poet whom it is impossible not to hear:

> Not in the hands of boys, but in their eyes
> Shall shine the holy glimmers of good-byes.
> The pallor of girls' brows shall be their pall;
> Their flowers the tenderness of silent minds,
> And each slow dusk a drawing-down of blinds.

There you have a poetry that is inescapable. It is as emphatic as poetry can be. But Owen, after passing through a period of hesitancy, had emerged finally into a poetry of direct statement that is only comparable, for its vigour, its freshness, and its tenacity, with that of such a forerunner of Augustan poetry as Rochester. It is too soon to be certain if the main body of modern poetry will follow in the same direction. Augustan poetry was mainly the creation of Dryden. But if Owen is our Rochester, who is tq be our Dryden ?

## II

The English spoken and written in the mid-nineteenth century was characterized, as we have seen, by diffuseness and vagueness. And the two qualities, it is clear, were interdependent. The diffuseness was a consequence of the vagueness. Two words were required to do the duty of one because a single word was so enveloped in emotional connotations that its meaning, its intellectual content, was never certain. But with the return of a greater precision to words the prolixity of Victorian English became obsolete and the language became terser and more concentrated. The change can be seen in the increasing succinctness of the letters, speeches, and newspaper articles of the period as well as in the diminishing rotundity of the spoken language as recorded in plays, novels, and *Punch*. We use fewer words than our fathers and grandfathers ; we are more direct ; we do not need to take their elaborate

Line 5. *For* comprable *read* comparable

precautions to ensure being understood. And our poetry has changed with our language.

The relative concision or diffuseness of a poetic style can be tested in the translations made in it. Here is one of the most successful and popular of the Victorian translations from the Greek Anthology —William Cory's 'Heraclitus':

They told me, Heraclitus, they told me you were dead,
They brought me bitter news to hear and bitter tears to
    shed.
I wept as I remember'd how often you and I
Had tired the sun with talking and sent him down the sky.

And now that thou art lying, my dear old Carian guest,
A handful of grey ashes, long, long ago at rest,
Still are thy pleasant voices, thy nightingales, awake;
For Death, he taketh all away, but them he cannot take.

And here is a translation, or adaptation, of another piece from the Greek Anthology by a modern poet:

    Bill Jupp lies 'ere, aged sixty year:
      From Tavistock 'e came.
    Single 'e bided, and 'e wished
      'Is father done the same.[1]

The two poems have been translated into literal prose by Dr. J. W. Mackail:[2]

One told me of thy fate, Heraclitus, and wrung me to tears, and I remembered how often both of us let the sun sink as we talked; but thou, methinks, O friend from Halicarnassus, art ashes long and long ago; yet thy nightin-

---

[1] L. A. G. Strong, *Dublin Days*, 1921, p. 23.
[2] *Select Epigrams from the Greek Anthology*, 1917, pp. 75, 64.

gale-notes live, whereon Hades the ravisher of all things shall not lay his hand.

I Dionysius of Tarsus lie here at sixty, having never married; and I would that my father had not.

It will be seen that the modern version contains practically the same number of words as the literal translation, whereas Cory's version is nearly twice as long. And the explanation of the difference is that Cory was not content to say anything once. 'Told' comes twice in his first line and 'bitter' twice in the second; 'they brought me news' is a repetition of 'they told me', and 'I wept' of 'tears to shed'; 'tired the sun' implies 'sent him down the sky'; and 'ashes' are generally 'a handful' and 'grey'. The modern version, on the other hand, adds nothing and subtracts nothing from the Greek.

The motive underlying the verbal and structural diffuseness of Victorian poetry can be put with brutal frankness. It was to write poetry as prose. It is a simple fact, easily verifiable by a paraphrase or translation, that the majority of the poems of Tennyson, Arnold, and the Brownings, and their imitators, can be read either as poetry or as prose. They possess, it is true, the verbal and metrical structure of poetry, but superimposed upon the poetic structure, and detachable from it, there is a framework of prose. A Victorian poem had a 'plot' (i.e. a beginning, a middle, and an end) : it narrated a story ; it described an incident ; it expounded an argument. And in order to satisfy the claims of prose the poetic cohesion had often to be sacrificed —as, for example, in Tennyson's 'The Sailor Boy':

He rose at dawn and, fired with hope,
   Shot o'er the seething harbour-bar,
And reach'd the ship and caught the rope,
   And whistled to the morning star.

And while he whistled long and loud
   He heard a fierce mermaiden cry,
'O boy, tho' thou art young and proud,
   I see the place where thou wilt lie.

'The sands and yeasty surges mix
   In caves about the dreary bay,
And on thy ribs the limpet sticks,
   And in thy heart the scrawl shall play.'

'Fool,' he answer'd, 'death is sure
   To those that stay and those that roam,
But I will nevermore endure
   To sit with empty hands at home.

'My mother clings about my neck,
   My sisters crying, "Stay for shame":
My father raves of death and wreck,
   They are all to blame, they are all to blame.

'God help me! save I take my part
   Of danger on the roaring sea,
A devil rises in my heart,
   Far worse than any death to me.'

What is wrong with Tennyson's poem, as poetry, is that it is 'thin'; it lacks body. And it is thin because it is too long. The poetry is unduly diluted. The simple process of omitting the second, fourth, and fifth verses—or, more drastically, of retaining only the third verse—would have improved things immensely. But Tennyson was telling a story as well as writing a poem, and a shorter poem would have spoilt his story. He had to choose between the claims of poetry and the claims of prose. The prose won.

The object, or at any rate the effect, of Tennyson's infusion of prose into poetry has been to make his poems easy to read. The common reader of to-day is a reader of prose. The verbal constructions that he is accustomed to encounter in print are those of the reporters and analysts of experience, and his normal reaction to the creator of experience—for so the poet may be defined—is one of bewilderment. The poet who is nothing but a poet speaks to him in a foreign language. The half-hidden relations between word and phrase out of which poetry is made are too intricate and unusual for him to follow. But Tennyson and the Victorian poets sugared the common reader's pill. The dramatic and narrative framework of their poems, by circumventing the disconcerting plunges into *medias res* which are of the essence of poetry, brings it down to the level of prose. The reader knows where he is; it serves the purpose of an introduction and notes. And in those poems—unfortunately they are not many—where the framework can be disregarded when it has fulfilled its explanatory function it may be held that no great harm is done.

The repetitions in Cory's 'Heraclitus', in so far as they are not simply emphatic, have a similar origin. They are the homage paid by poetry to prose *within* the poem. Their effect, that is, is to smooth over and explain away the abrupt transitions and metaphorical language of poetry. (A phrase is never so formidable if it is followed by a paraphrase.) And the reader, who might otherwise have taken fright and bolted, continues reassured. It was a favourite device of Tennyson's in *In Memoriam* :

> Sleep, gentle winds, as he sleeps now,
> My friend, the brother of my love ;

> My Arthur, whom I shall not see
> Till all my widow'd race be run ;
> Dear as the mother to the son,
> More than my brothers are to me.

Evidently 'the brother of my love' was too bold a phrase to stand by itself; hence the next four lines, leading up to the gloss of 'More than my brothers are to me'.

The poems of Robert Bridges and Mr. A. E. Housman—who may be taken to represent respectively the first and second generation after Tennyson—are markedly less dependent on prose. A certain deficiency in firmness and vividness may be admitted in Bridges. There are still occasional otiose repetitions and explanations,[1] and the transitions are unnecessarily smooth and logical. But, though the diction was never quite strong enough to impose its own form, there is little evidence of an alien prosaic framework. Bridges's poems do not tell stories or inculcate morals, and the incidents related—as in 'Indolence'—are not dramatized or elaborated as

---

[1] In 'London Snow', perhaps Bridges's best poem, 'falling' (l. 2) explains 'flying' (l. 1), and 'Hushing' (l. 4) is explained by 'Deadening, muffling, stifling' (l. 5).

they would have been by Tennyson and Browning One imagines that the diction Bridges inherited— already devitalized by Pre-Raphaelite excesses—was too feeble and flaccid for a bolder treatment to have been possible. Mr. Housman's *A Shropshire Lad* and *Last Poems* have the firmness of outline that Bridges's poems generally lacked, but it has been obtained by a reversion to a prosaic framework. The majority of the poems are epigrams in the form, if not the spirit, of Martial, and the Latin epigram, with its insistence on 'point', is essentially a kind of prose. (It is 'progressive' rather than 'esemplastic'.) Mr. Housman, it is true, has succeeded in introducing some admirably vivid phrases into his epigrams—it will be by his gift of phrase that he will survive—but their framework, the structural norm, is prose.

It is only recently, in the work of writers like Wilfred Owen, Mr. Robert Graves, and Mr. W. H. Auden,[1] that a poetry has arisen which has been wholly divorced from prose. This poetry has been labelled 'difficult'. It is possible, however, that much of its difficulty is due simply to its having discarded those prosaic elements which readers have been accustomed to expect in modern poetry. Poetry *is* more difficult than prose—for the habitual reader of prose. But is Mr. Auden's 'Epilogue' more difficult than Shakespeare's poetry or Blake's?

---

[1] I am deliberately omitting to consider Mr. W. B. Yeats and Mr. T. S. Eliot. The one is an Irishman, the other an American, and the language they maltreat with masterly virtuosity is not exactly English but a sweeter and less stubborn instrument, a *dead* language.

'O where are you going?' said reader to rider,
'That valley is fatal when furnaces burn,
Yonder's the midden whose odours will madden,
That gap is the grave where the tall return.'

'O do you imagine,' said fearer to farer,
'That dusk will delay on your path to the pass,
Your diligence looking discover the lacking,
Your footsteps feel from granite to grass?'

'O what was that bird,' said horror to hearer,
'Did you see that shape in the twisted trees?
Behind you swiftly the figure comes softly,
That spot on your skin is a shocking disease.'

'Out of this house,'—said rider to reader,
'Yours never will'—said farer to fearer,
'They're looking for you'—said hearer to horror
As he left them there, as he left them there.

Mr. Auden's poems, difficult or not, are an encouraging portent. For here for the first time since
the death of Keats are poems with a structure, solid
as the structures of prose, that has *not* been superimposed. The coherence of 'Epilogue' is an inner
poetic coherence, built up out of the direct relations
of phrase to phrase and word to word, and independent of external framework or internal explanatory phrases. Poetic form is not everything,
but it has become so rare in recent English literature
that Mr. Auden's achievement is worth more than
a passing salute. But it is perhaps premature to
attempt to relate that achievement to contemporary
conditions of speech.

Line 7. *For* your diligence *read* your diligent

Line 12. *For* That spot *read* The spot

Line 21. *For* coherence of 'Epilogue' is an inner poetic coherence
*read* coherence of this 'Epilogue' to *The Orators* is inner